The

GATE

of

BEAUTIFUL

Stories, Songs, and Reflections
ON CHRISTIAN LIFE

GERALD RASMUSSEN

Outskirts Press, Inc.
Denver, Colorado

Acknowledgments

It's difficult to know where to start in thanking those who have made this book possible.

All gifts come from the Lord, and without him I couldn't string together a complete sentence, let alone write a book. I first came to know and love Jesus hearing my mother tell me stories about him from the Bible. Her faith was an inspiration for me throughout her life, and continues to be to this day.

My spiritual growth has been nurtured by several ministers who have given generously of their time, patiently answering my endless questions. Many years ago, Reverend Dennis Albrecht, my pastor at St. John's Lutheran Church in Stamford, Connecticut, encouraged me to first start putting my thoughts down on paper. Some of those letters and our conversations over breakfast have been the basis of chapters in this book. In more recent years, Reverend Ken Smith of First Baptist Church, and Pastor Lou Santoro of Grace Bible Church, both in Shelton, Connecticut, have inspired me to continue my writing.

After performing folk and original music for many years, with only an occasional gospel song thrown in, my life was dramatically changed when Dan Williams, Director of the Men's Chorus at Union Baptist Church in Stamford, Connecticut, invited me to join the chorus. Dan's faith in me and his constant encouragement led me to form the Gospel Messengers from friends in the chorus. Joseph Evans, Franklin Cummings, and Derrick Hanchard were not only members of the quartet, they were wonderful, supportive friends who were always there for me. Many of the songs included in this book were written for the Gospel Messengers.

Miriam Hospodar, a wonderful writer from the West Coast, encouraged me to draw together my writings and songs into this book. As I was writing this book, I shared chapters with my friends and family, and their appreciation and encouragement gave me continuing inspiration.

Reverend Marcia C. Eveland and the trustees of First Congregational Church in Ansonia, Connecticut, graciously allowed me to use the photo of the beautiful gate of their church on the cover of this book.

My loving wife, Ruth, has been a gracious sounding board for my writings, and our readings and conversations over breakfast were a great blessing. She has always supported my efforts to serve the Lord.

All these people and many more have made the difference. There is no way I can adequately thank them for their gift of encouragement.

Contents

Scriptures quoted are from the
King James Version of the Bible unless otherwise noted.

Introduction

This One's for You, Jesus

Letters are the poor second cousins of literature. "Writers" write books. People write letters. Or used to. But letters weren't always thought of as just a way of keeping in touch with Aunt Maude. They are the heart and soul of the Bible. In the days of the apostles, letters were the lifeblood of the early church. We call them Epistles now. Epistles are just letters all dressed up in their Sunday go-to-meeting clothes. They rarely talked about the weather or about how Uncle Charlie backed into a light post and took out the left taillight. Merriam-Webster defines an epistle as: "A composition in the form of a letter." We tend to think of epistles more in terms of the primary definition, "one of the letters adopted as books of the New Testament." My old friend Reverend Dennis Albrecht believes that epistles are still being written today. I'd have to agree with him on that. It doesn't make sense to me that God stopped speaking through people after the Bible was written. He still speaks through us.

I started writing in high school. In tenth grade I had a poem published in *The Bluebird*—an annual collection of the best writing of the class. But I certainly didn't think of myself as a writer. I just wrote a poem because we were required to. I wrote my first song back in the early '50s—"Foam Rubber Dice." It was a doo-wop song, and the only thing I remember now is a nice bass part singing "foam rubber dice." When I went off to college I started writing letters. They definitely were not epistles. But, over the years, my letter writing, my song writing, and my faith merged. By the '60s I was writing profusely. I wrote because I loved to write, whether it was a letter, a song, or an occasional article for a folk music newsletter.

i

Through the '80s and for many years beyond, I shared almost daily correspondence with my friend Art Thieme. Although Art is an agnostic, much of what I wrote about was my growing exploration of my faith. By the '90s, I was regularly writing what I referred to as "Dear Dennis" letters to Reverend Dennis Albrecht, my pastor at that time. I found letter writing to be a good way to clarify my thinking about my faith, and the letters formed the foundation of many long discussions I had with Dennis over breakfast at Friendly's Restaurant. I started sharing copies of those letters with friends who I thought would enjoy them, and at one point had fifteen or sixteen people on my "Subscription" list.

With "Foam Rubber Dice," the floodgates were opened, and without ever setting out to do so, I became a songwriter. At first the songs were about small town life, blending my memories with those of my family. Occasionally, a gospel song would come out. In the '80s, I received a call from Field Horne inviting me to perform at the Appalachian Folk Gospel Festival. I was taken by surprise as I didn't think of myself as a gospel singer. Field had heard me do a concert at Cafe Lena in Saratoga Springs, NY, and while I only did a couple of gospel songs, he said that my faith was evident in all the songs I'd written. I ended up performing at that festival for the next three years until it ended. The Lord had this one all worked out. My letters were taking on the character of epistles, and my songwriting was turning more and more toward gospel.

Which brings me to this book. It wasn't my idea. The Lord moved me to draw together some of my letters, writings, and songs to share with others. When the Lord tells me to do something, I do it—at least most of the time. Back in 1997, he moved me to start a gospel quartet—The Gospel Messengers. In the beginning, we sang mostly old black gospel music. Through the years, our repertoire subtly shifted toward the gospel songs that I wrote for the group. Along the way, my letters, writings, and gospel songs became so interwoven that I could no longer separate them. That's why they are all a part of this book.

If nothing ever came of writing this book, it still would have been a great blessing to me. As I've gone along, I've shared chapters with family and friends, and their enthusiasm and encouragement gave me the determination to keep writing. As it always has, writing this book has strengthened my understanding of my faith. It has kept me firmly rooted in the Bible, and I have often felt Jesus by my side. For me, writing is worship and prayer. And so, I do this for the Lord. This one's for you, Jesus.

I Was Talking with God the Other Day

God talks to us in many ways. Sometimes, it isn't until much later that we realize that it was God. More often than not, words aren't involved. One day, I was driving in my car, deeply depressed. It was an overcast, foreboding day, which wasn't doing a lot for my spirits. As I came around a curve in the street, a single beam of sunlight cut through the clouds, brilliantly illuminating a mailbox. The name on the mailbox was Goodson, but one of the O's was missing, making it Godson. And not a word was spoken. You just have to know the language.

My wife, Ruth, and I were in Wisconsin visiting my family, and we'd gone out to dinner with my son Aaron. I don't remember how the subject came up, but Aaron asked me, "What do you mean when you say that God told you something?" It was a question on his mind, asked respectfully. Aaron is an agnostic, but we've always had good conversations about my faith, a faith that Aaron once had as a child. It was a good question, worthy of a thoughtful answer. Essentially, he was asking, what is prayer?

Too often, people think of prayer as asking God for something. It may be something for good, like the healing of a loved one, or the strength to do a task set before us. But, prayer is much more than asking. If that was all it was, that would assume that we are wise enough to know what to ask for. As often as not, we aren't. Sometimes, the most loving answer that God can give us when we ask for something is "no." He knows what's good for us far more than we do. There's a difference between talking to God and talking *with* God. Prayer is a two-way street. Listening is as important as talking. Sometimes our conversation is like the lines I wrote in a song many years ago:

We'd sit and we'd talk till there's no more to say
But we never needed words, anyway[1]

And that's the way that it is with God. Silence is a natural part of a conversation with a close friend. Every available moment doesn't have to be filled with words. God often speaks without words when we are silently waiting for him to speak to us. This is how I tried to explain to Aaron of how God speaks to me. In biblical times, God sometimes spoke out loud, as he did to Moses. He also sent angels (Gabriel usually got the call) to deliver a message for him. Most of us don't "hear" God speak in a stentorian (offscreen) voice. And while I do believe there are times when angels are sent to tell us something, they may not speak out loud, and they can come in the form of a person, minus the wings.

Many years ago, when I was in a state of depression, caught in a trap of my own making, I was walking down the street in Stamford, Connecticut, where I was living at the time. My head was hung low and as I was walking along deep in thought, I heard a little girl singing. I looked up, and skipping down the sidewalk toward me was a young girl singing "A Mighty Fortress Is Our God" at the top of her lungs. It took a moment to sink in, and by then she'd passed me. I turned around to look at her and the street was empty. A few weeks later, I was walking down that same street and when I came to the place where I'd seen the young girl, I was reminded of that day. At that moment, the carillon tower in the church down the block started playing "A Mighty Fortress Is Our God." There were no burning bushes, and no words spoken, and yet God spoke to me clearly. Not to worry. God is a mighty fortress. He's in the business of solving problems, if we just take them to him. God speaks to us. He doesn't have to shout.

When I am in prayer, it is in the times of silence that God speaks to me. He may direct me to do something as simple as call an old friend whom I haven't spoken to in a long time, or to sit down and write about something that he has put on my mind. More commonly, God gives me a new insight into an old problem. At first, I may not understand what he is saying to me. I get the message, but not the

---

[1] "Winter to Spring"

meaning. It may take days or weeks, or even months of prayer, reflection, and reading the Bible before I fully understand what he is trying to tell me. Revelation comes slowly. I've learned to wait on the Lord for his enlightenment before I step out in faith.

Every parent at some time or another has complained, "My kids never call me!" God must feel the same way. If we want to come to know God, it can't be on a "use as needed" basis. We have to spend time in daily prayer and reflection. Oswald Chambers, in his book *My Utmost for His Highest,* wrote: "The only responsibility you have is to stay in living constant touch with God and to see that you allow nothing to hinder your cooperation with him."

Many years ago I spent a summer studying about the Holy Spirit under the guidance of my pastor. I spent an enormous amount of time reading, meditating, praying, and just spending time with the Lord in silence. I ended up boiling down that whole summer of reflection into a single sentence: "Something tells me that the something that tells me something is the Holy Spirit."

If you want to hear God, ask him to speak to you, and then be quiet.

A Bus Story

*I*f we could see through the eyes of Jesus, what a different world would unfold before us. If we had Christ's compassion, we could experience the world as he did. I envision Christ watching our foolishness and clumsy attempts at holiness with the same love, compassion, and humor that a parent has watching their child take his or her first hesitant steps. He can see our determination, our weakness, and our childish simplicity. It's not that he would laugh at our efforts to be like him. But he certainly would smile lovingly, and approve of our efforts, however misguided they may be at times. Sometimes we are privileged to see the world around us through Christ's eyes and with his compassion, and we see how beautiful people are, despite all their failings.

This story comes from a bus trip my wife and I took from Minneapolis to South Dakota in 2004. By the time we boarded the bus in Minneapolis, we were already exhausted from a long bus ride up from Janesville, Wisconsin, with a change of buses in Madison. But let me tell you the story. Read it with Christ's eyes, as I saw it.

She got on in Minneapolis. I was sitting in the aisle seat, and she came in and sat down on the aisle seat across from me, one row in front of us. We hadn't even left the station before she turned and started talking to me and my wife. At first, it was a three-way conversation, but we'd been on the road for most of the day and soon my wife scrunched down into her chair and closed her eyes, and the woman was just talking to me. She looked like she was probably in her mid or late forties, and her face looked lived in. Every line had a story. She introduced herself as Sherri, and was noticeably shaken when I told her my name was Jerry. "I'm an identical twin," she said. "My sister's name was Jerry. She died a long time ago, and I still miss talking to her. She was always there when I needed her."

Sherri was on the last leg of a long trip. She was on her way to see her husband, and she poured out her life story. She met her husband when she was just eighteen, and they got married a couple of weeks after they met. Four years after their daughter was born, they split up and separated. Sherri didn't give any reason why . . . not because she was inhibited, but because she was talking with such immediacy that the words were just tumbling out of her. After she left her husband, she went through several other relationships and in recent years had been living with a man who was on drugs and was treating her like she was disposable. He was openly having an affair with another woman, which Sherri had accepted for a long time. She had even helped the woman he was having an affair with get a job where she worked, and had helped her out financially. She felt trapped with the man and wanted to get out, but he kept threatening her about what he'd do if she left. Among other things, he said he'd have her dog put to sleep. But finally, Sherri had to accept that she'd have to take that chance.

Sherri reached the point where she was so depressed that she told her parents everything. She didn't want to go back to live with them because they had no money or room for her, so she had nowhere to go. She just knew that she couldn't go on living the way that she was. Her parents told her that they'd give her bus fare if she wanted to go back to her husband. It had been twenty-one years since she'd spoken to him, but she was able to track down a phone number and called him. She asked if she could come back and live with him, and he told her that he'd never stopped loving her. As she talked to me, the pain and stress in her voice and whole body started to soften. She realized that no one had ever treated her as well as her husband had. He told her that he didn't look the same anymore, and she assured him that she didn't either. But, they were excited about getting back together, and he would have a chance to meet his daughter, who was now twenty-five and had very little memory of him.

Late that afternoon, as the prairie sun was starting to set, our bus stopped at a small bus station in the middle of nowhere. Sherry got up and nervously tugged on the small travel bag she'd wedged into the overhead luggage rack. She was traveling light. There was no attempt to put on her best face or check her hair in the mirror. She was plainly dressed, in old blue jeans and a simple shirt-top, with plain brown shoes. We could sense her uncertainty as she stepped down from the bus. There to greet her was a short, red-haired man, gone a little wide in the body over the years. His blue jeans and plaid shirt complemented hers, and he fidgeted, waiting to see how she would respond. They met right outside our window, and you could see a moment of hesitation and uncertainty in their eyes. Would the other person be disappointed? Would they regret agreeing to come back together? It was a fleeting moment, and then she dove into his outstretched arms, and the smiles on their faces were beatific. What an honor for us to witness such joy! We looked over at each other, our grins matching those of the couple standing outside our window. Even though the bus door had closed and we couldn't hear anything they were saying, we could see the excitement in their eyes and the way that they touched each other, and you could see that they were both talking a mile a minute. They had a lot of catching up to do.

Blessings for Breakfast

*E*arly in the morning as you lie there in bed, suspended between the last dream of the night and the dawning of a new day, God comes calling. If you listen carefully, you will hear him. He speaks in a small, still voice. It is in the intimacy of those first precious moments that God reveals himself to you. If you spend time abiding in him, you will arise from your bed of rest to a breakfast of blessings.

There is something holy about that awakening hour. It is no surprise that God has often chosen that time to make himself known to his people. God, in speaking to Aaron and Miriam, called them:

> And they both came forth. And he said, "Hear now my words; if there be a prophet among you, I the Lord will make myself known unto him in a vision, and will speak unto him in a dream." (Numbers 12:5–6)

God still speaks to us in the same way. When we lie there, drifting in and out of sleep, all of the defenses and rationalizations of our waking hours are still at rest. In biblical times, visions were considered holy and a direct announcement from God. Visionaries were revered as the wisest of prophets. Those days have sadly passed away. Visionaries are now more likely to be looked upon as delusional. Merriam-Webster defines a visionary as "one whose ideas or projects are impractical," and "existing only in imagination: unreal." That's hardly complimentary. Interestingly though, there is one positive definition of a visionary: "As in the computer industry." It's clear who and what is worshipped, these days. When someone says, "In your dreams," it's a put-down: "Yeah, right . . . in your dreams." Dreams have been relegated to carnival sideshows and readers of palms, not Psalms.

For all the denigration of dreams and visions, that awakening time is often one of great clarity where God speaks to us with his wisdom, not that of man's. It is a time of revelation. With all the pressures and distractions of the coming day still before you, that early morning oasis can also be a time of creativity. Once your heels hit the floor, the demands of the day make reflection a luxury that most of us can't afford. We have to catch God on the run. But there in the early morning quiet, your mind is free to go wherever the Lord takes you. Many years ago I awakened to write a song, describing that early morning peace.

Softly, the morning moves over the wall
Warming the bed where we lay
Soft golden colors, they turn and they spin
Welcome another new day[2]

That song came to me as I lay in bed watching the sunlight slowly moving across the wall. While lingering dreams color those first moments of a new day, lines to a new song often form in my mind. It was on such an early morning, the day after I'd been deeply moved by an elderly woman in a nursing home, when I sang a line that suddenly came to me:

And somewhere inside her, there's still that young girl
With a tortoiseshell comb in her hair[3]

It is because of those early morning inspirations that I used to keep a pad and pen next to my bed so that when the Lord put something on my heart, I could roll over and write it down. Now that we've "advanced" to computers, I have to rustle myself out of the warmth of the bed and head downstairs to my office and fire up Microsoft Word. The process remains the same. God talks to me in times of peaceful reflection and gives me a line of a new song, or

---

[2] "Softly, the Morning"
[3] "Tortoiseshell Comb"

something that he wants me to write about. He gives a new meaning to the term "Wake-Up Call."

Like many others, I love the hymn, "Order My Steps." That early morning time with the Lord is Step-Ordering time. If in our heart we truly desire to do God's will, what better time is there to ask for his guidance than the beginning of a new day? If we allow God to order our steps, we will arise with a clarity of purpose. The sun beams slanting in through the window will have a new radiance, as if we've never seen a sunrise before. The aroma of the freshly-brewed coffee will fill the kitchen, and the birds outside the window will sing the promise of a brand new day.

And when we sit at the table for our morning breakfast, we will be overwhelmed with thanksgiving for the many blessings of the day.

Transcendent

*J*ust *when you think you've got everything figured out, the Lord steps in and surprises you. Sometimes, the most unpromising situations turn out to be the most fruitful. This was one of those nights.*

It was a dark and rainy night, and very foggy, too. I was scheduled to do a concert and I was concerned about driving, but I bravely drove off into the murky Connecticut night. I didn't hold out much hope of getting an audience, and I wasn't disappointed. The concert was scheduled to start at eight p.m., and by the time eight o'clock rolled around, there was no one there except for the people who ran the concert series and the sound. There's a "death watch" mood that settles in when that happens. No matter how much good-natured kidding around there is, everyone is privately thinking, "Why am I doing this?" At five after eight, a young couple arrived and we had an audience. They were mock-cheered as they came through the doorway. After that, the audience trickled in. There finally were two couples, three men who came alone, and three women who also came alone.

When everyone sat down, they scattered around the room so that there was no sense of being an audience. Even the first couple that arrived didn't sit next to each other. After doing the first two or three songs and getting very little response from the audience, I knew that I was in for a long night. People weren't singing along on the choruses, and everyone seemed very self-conscious. But I plugged along.

As the first set wore on, there were signs that people were loosening up and responding to the music. There was a woman, probably in her mid or upper sixties who was sitting alone who would close her eyes, tilt her head back, and sway gently from side to side in rhythm with the songs. The blank, unconvinced expressions that greeted the first few songs were slowly replaced by smiles and laughter. I ended the first set with a song I had written a month or so earlier with the chorus:

For the good old days are still to come
Though the hard times are not over
For we must wear that thorny crown
To walk the fields of clover[4]

After I finished the song, I got down from the stage and was immediately challenged by a question that was hurled at me, "Why do Christians think that you have to suffer?" I was caught off guard by the question because the song made no explicit reference to Christianity. I guess the thorny crown was the giveaway. I responded by saying that I don't think that most Christians think you *have* to suffer. They just recognize that suffering is a part of the tapestry of our lives, whatever our religious beliefs. Christians don't have a corner on suffering. And, as I pointed out, the chorus to the song is most reflective of my friend Art Thieme's philosophy about suffering, and he is Jewish. Suddenly, over coffee and brownies, we were off on a raging discussion about suffering.

Then someone else chimed in that not all Christians believe you have to suffer. I tried not to get too preachy because I didn't want to get into a discussion about religion. I could have said that Christ's suffering gives Christians hope, knowing that he can understand what we are going through, but I didn't. Instead, I focused on another line of the song that gives suffering a more positive meaning, "For all the burdens that we share, let us lift our voice in praise." The depth of a relationship has everything to do with our burdens, and that had certainly been true for Art and me.

In the second set, I did three songs that pulled the audience together to the point that, after the concert, one of the men who arrived alone said, "We were talking about the cycle of life."

The first song I did is very fragmentary, about three different

---

[4] "Fields of Clover"

people in wheelchairs whom I'd sung for in a nursing home. One of the women was so severely paralyzed that she was strapped into her wheelchair. The only movement she could make was lifting one finger, which she tapped in rhythm to the songs. There was no smile on her face because it was completely paralyzed. That night, I had a dream about that woman, and there was a song in the dream with the line, "And somewhere inside her there's still that young girl, with a tortoiseshell comb in her hair." After singing the song, I talked a little about the other people I'd visited with at the nursing home that same day. I told them about an elderly man in a wheelchair who was so weak he couldn't shake my hand, although he tried. When he talked about his life, he took pride in saying that he'd always been good with his hands (another line in the song). A few songs later, I did another song I'd written, "Lavender Ladies," and talked about the devastating blow for a woman when her husband suddenly dies and all the dreams of their lifetimes are shattered. The song also talks about the men who found so much of their value in their work, whether they were corporate executives or common laborers, like my father. It seems like "keeping busy" is the ultimate goal of retirement for most men. And then I asked, "What about the women who lose their husbands?" A line from the song asks, "Where are the men who can find their contentment in a living room waltz or a walk by the sea?"

I finished the concert with another song I'd written, "Handful of Songs." In introducing the song, I talked abut those things that we leave behind that are of the greatest value. The song speaks of my grandfather's hammer and his old railroad watch, which I claimed after his death, and "The Bible my grandmother bought her last Christmas, that she gave to my mother," when my mother was just thirteen years old. I told them about a friend of mine whose prize remembrance of his father is a hockey puck his father caught as it flew into the stands when my friend was just a boy, sitting there filled with pride when his father handed it to him. The hockey puck has a place of honor on top of his dresser. When you get right down to it, what is of lasting value? Anything that was loved. My mother always said that life is making memories, so we should try to make them as good as we can.

When I finished the concert, several people came up to talk with me. Usually, they want to say how much they enjoyed a particular song, or to ask me if I know a song that they like, but not that night.

The first comments someone made came from the man who said, "We were talking about the cycle of life." He works with crippled children, and he saw the common thread between them and the elderly people strapped in wheelchairs. The cycle of life comes full circle from being physically dependent as a child, to the frailty and weakness of the elderly. He described the look of complete joy on the face of a young crippled boy who he lifted up to sit on the back of a horse on a field trip a few weeks earlier. He recognized the common spirit in that young boy who could only express himself with a smile, and the paralyzed woman who could only gently tap one finger. And he knew, seeing that smile on the boy's face, that "somewhere inside" him he was filled with joy and thanksgiving that the man had helped him to sit on the back of that horse. And the floodgates opened. Everyone had a story to tell. What followed was a warm, open sharing among a group of strangers who began the night sitting far away from each other, responding guardedly to my music and conversation. A group of us stood there talking, with me listening, mostly.

The first man, who'd spoken about the cycle of life, said that when we are young and physically vital, we deal with matters of the body: the pleasure of exercise, sports, sex, being good with our hands, working—all the fulfilling activities that go with a strong, healthy body. As we get older and lose that physical vitality, we turn more toward matters of the mind and heart, to a more spiritual life. He talked about the loss for people who are denied the richness of that cycle of life, who die when they are still young. By this time, others were entering the conversation. A couple with a daughter in her early twenties talked about the difficulty of remaining close to her as she was breaking away from them and establishing her own life, a part of the cycle of life they were really struggling with.

As we talked, everyone offered their own limited insights and feelings. One man in his forties (who had arrived and sat alone) talked about how hard it was for him to regain any closeness or understanding of his father as an adult after his father had died. His father had been a doctor, and the young man had saved a penlight that his father had used in giving medical examinations. And then, as the conversation continued to flow, a man talked about a woman he worked with who was recently widowed and was having a hard time adjusting to her loss. She was at retirement age, and the business where they worked was "encouraging" her to retire by giving her all the most difficult, unpleasant jobs. Despite that, she was the one who remembered everyone's birthday and brought in cookies and cakes that she baked for them. I shared conversations that I'd had with widowed women who had defined themselves solely as mothers and wives. They were having a hard time accepting that, with their children grown up, they were no longer needed as mothers. My response was that they would always be needed as mothers, but their role in "mothering" was over. Then, when their husbands died, they suddenly weren't wives any more. That led to a discussion about the necessity of redefining ourselves. That's something that happens many times in our lives, not just when we are old.

And then we talked about facing death. (This was just a folk concert, not a marathon study group.) We talked about the comfort that many elderly people have, accepting death as an approaching reality. Several people had their own observations about how people who are elderly have made their transition so beautifully from the physically vital stage in their cycle of life to a more spiritual plane. I talked about my father and his ability to give thanks for still being able to walk with a walker. Although he was slowly losing more of his strength, he was still thankful for the strength he had.

As we stood there talking, I think we all realized that something very rare was happening. We had transcended the isolation of our lives and were deeply engaged in sharing our most personal thoughts and fears with a group of people who entered the room as strangers. Finally, it was time to leave. While I hadn't fully understood what had happened in that flowing conversation, I had enough sense to know that I wanted to hold on to it, a feeling very much like the one you have when you wake from a beautiful dream and want to go to sleep to reimmerse yourself.

When I got home, I tried to understand what had happened. I couldn't say I was overwhelmed by the experience because it was very subtle and quiet. I couldn't accurately describe it by saying I had a "great" evening. What would that mean? "Transcendent" seemed to be the only word that fit. Somehow, a group of strangers were swept away and for a few minutes shared their deepest reflections on their lives and the lives of those they love or work with. The man who said, "We were talking about the cycle of life," was right. We were, even though not a word was spoken by anyone but me until the break, and then after the concert. It was a conversation with one finger tapping.

The Black Sparrow

*B*ack in the Bible days, folks were always looking for signs. God gave Noah the rainbow sign as proof of his new covenant:

And I establish my covenant with you; neither shall all flesh be cut off any more by the waters of a flood; neither shall there any more be a flood to destroy the earth. And God said, this is the token of the covenant which I make between me and you and every living creature that is with you, for perpetual generations. I do set my bow in the cloud, and it shall be for a token of a covenant between me and the earth. (Genesis 9:11–13)

People needed to see, to believe. Christ became frustrated with those who followed him, always looking for signs and miracles:

And then Jesus said unto them, Except ye see signs and wonders, ye will not believe. (John 4:48)

Like those who followed Christ over two thousand years ago, we look for signs, too. We may not expect to see God in a burning bush, or interpret a comet as a word from God, but we still turn to him, looking for guidance. Sometimes he speaks to us in ways that we never would expect. This was one of those times.

The fall of 1997 was a time of great confusion for me. At that time, I was a member of a Lutheran church with a Scandinavian heritage, and it fit my need to worship very comfortably. I was baptized by my Uncle Harold, who was a Lutheran minister, and my grandfather and grandmother Rasmussen were Lutheran. A year earlier I had been asked by my pastor to open the church for the

Men's Chorus of the black Baptist Church across the road. Their church was under construction and the Lutheran church offered the use of their sanctuary for practice for an upcoming concert. I always had a great love for black gospel, and when I heard the Men's Chorus, I was overwhelmed. In the ensuing year, I went to hear them whenever I could and was invited to join the Chorus. For awhile I attended both churches every Sunday morning, but the time came when I had to make a choice between them. While I loved the Lutheran church, I felt God was leading me to join the Baptist church where I was singing. What I needed was a sign. Not that I prayed for one, exactly. But, God gave me one anyway. In those days, I went for a daily walk "In the Garden." I had come to rely on my walks as a time when I could draw close to the Lord and look to him for guidance. My "garden" was the neighborhood where I was living at the time. I came to the garden alone, seeking that closeness with Jesus that the song so beautifully captures.

On this particular morning I had a remarkable experience that I recounted in a letter to my dear friend, Art Thieme.

"Hi, Art: Through all of this, Art, I think that we have just been reminded that, on matters of faith, we are beholden to no one else. I'm sorry that I've disrupted people's lives, but it's hard to sustain a real funk when I am so *delighted* with my own spiritual revival. I've got to tell you a story, Art—a true story. It happened to me yesterday. Yesterday morning, I woke up with the chorus to a song in my head. It may never become a song, but there it was, and after running it through my head a few times, the first couple of lines of a verse came out. The song in itself isn't important, so I'll not even bother to put the lines down in this letter. The song came out because I was feeling such frustration because there is a wedge coming between me and people I really care about, even though we share the same basic faith.

"When I went for my morning walk, the song was buzzing around in my head. Halfway through the walk, I passed the Catholic church where I was married (*my first marriage*). It's on my walk, so I pass it every day. It just turned out that there was a morning Mass (this was Columbus Day) and it was just getting over. On the spur of the moment, I decided to stop in and say a few prayers. I felt the

20

need to take a few minutes to talk with the Lord about my situation, seeking guidance from him.

"Walking back, I was lost in thought about all that's been happening to me, when I noticed a sparrow on the lawn next to the sidewalk, no more than three feet away from me. I was walking on a heavily traveled, noisy street, so I was surprised that the sparrow would be standing there so calmly. I would have expected that he would have flown away long before I got that close to him. He looked to be healthy and downright plump, if anything, so I didn't think that there was anything wrong with him. There was something unusual about him, though. He was completely black: a black beak, even black legs. He had very sleek, beautiful black feathers, as black as a crow, but much more lustrous. I've seen black squirrels and an albino sparrow, but I've never seen a black sparrow. I was taken aback by the whole experience. So, I said, 'Good morning, Mister Sparrow! and how are you on this beautiful day?' (I had been reading Uncle Remus, and it was only later that I realized that I was in a Tar Baby situation.) And Mister Sparrow, he said nothing. But he didn't hop away. He looked me straight in the eye and cocked his head to the side. He took a little sideways hop or two but made no effort to leave. So I asked him straight out, 'Why aren't you flying away?' And Mister Sparrow, he said nothing. And then it hit me. I suppose the connection was understandable.

I was so immersed in reaching out to a black church and causing so much consternation because of it that it made sense that I'd be carrying on a conversation with a black sparrow. So, I asked the only other logical question I could think of. 'Did you come from God?' Hey, Moses saw God in a burning bush. There are all sorts of southern folk traditions about spirits appearing in the form of a bird. The Holy Ghost descended from heaven as a white dove. Leave it to me to have him appear as a black sparrow. But Mr. Sparrow didn't have anything to tell me, Art. He just casually hopped across the sidewalk, three feet away from me. He was in no hurry. And then he hopped under a hedge. As I stood there in the brilliant fall sunlight, tears welled up in my eyes, and I said to myself, 'Praise Jesus!' 'Thank you, Jesus.'

"Was it a sign? Was God trying to tell me that I should pursue my embracing of Union Baptist Church? Or was it just a black sparrow? It's kind of hard to come up with any empirical answer to that one. Personally, I took it as a sign. 'His eye is on the sparrow.' "

For the record, I taught bird classes for several years, and there is no such thing as a black sparrow. After this experience, I looked in every bird book I had, and they don't exist. Tell that to Mister Sparrow.

Pre-hindsight

*T*here's no surprising God.

A few years ago, I got into a long discussion with a friend of mine on this topic. He knew how many unexpected changes had occurred in my life and he said, "God must really be surprised at how your life is turning out." My response was, "You can't surprise God; he's omniscient. He knows everything I'm going to do even before I do it." There's no such thing as being pretty-darned omniscient. Either you're omniscient or you aren't. God is the only true know-it-all. He knows what's going to happen in the future. My friend countered that "If God knows what we're going to do in the future, then we don't have free will." And I answered, "Just because God knows what we're going to do in the future doesn't mean that we don't have the freedom to do it."

Time is a human concept. God sees everything at once. For us mortals, we see our life in the rearview mirror. We have to wait for hindsight. When our life seems to be crashing down around us and we start to lose heart, we can take comfort in the Word.

And we know that all things work together for good to them that love God, to them who are called according to His purpose. (Romans 8:28)

But, being human, there have been times when I've prayed to God to reveal to me how the hard times in my life are really working "together for good." I can be pretty impatient, sometimes. This was written, remembering one of those times in my life when I couldn't afford to wait for hindsight.

We all can look back at hard times in our lives and see that they were blessings in disguise. But sometimes, when life is most stressful, hindsight takes too long. We need pre-hindsight. I remember a particularly difficult time in my first marriage when I prayed to God for pre-hindsight. At the time, I was driving an old Pinto.

> *I drive an old Pinto, gone long in the tooth*
> *Known by every mechanic from here to Duluth*[5]

The floor boards were rotted so badly that only a couple of two-by-fours I'd wedged between the seat and the frame of the car kept me from falling through the floor onto the highway. At least it was easy to keep my eye on the road. All I had to do was look through the holes in the floor.

On this particular day my Pinto was in the garage, and I was walking to work. It was a five-mile walk, and I was already stressed out from a battle-zone marriage and endless financial problems. As I was walking along talking with God, I asked Him, "All right, God. . . where are all the blessings in this?" I couldn't wait another six months to find out. I wouldn't survive that long. As I was passing a newly built house, I did a double-take, and then laughed out loud. The groundhog had built a swell new house, right next to the new building. The ground was soft and house was finished, but no one had moved in yet, except for the new resident in the yard. A perfect spot for digging a burrow. There was a mound of dirt in front of the entry hole he'd dug, and it was a beautiful day, so the groundhog was out sunning himself on his veranda. I called over to him and wished him a good day.

After I rounded the corner, I was walking on the side of the road on a street without a sidewalk. There was a car approaching me, and I noticed a dog that was running "hell bent for leather" alongside it. As the car came closer, I realized the dog didn't see me and was about to run me over. At the last moment, he skidded to a halt, looking somewhat chagrined, and looked up at me apologetically, waiting for a good ear scratch. It was then that I realized why he hadn't seen me. He was blind in his right eye. He ended up as one

---

[5] "I Drive an Old Pinto," by Jerry Rasmussen

verse in a song I wrote:

Though he'd lost the vision in his right eye
He would always keep his left eye on the road[6]

What could I do but praise the Lord? He had blessed me with a good, hearty laugh, a verse for a song, and the pre-hindsight to see that even though I had no idea how I was going to survive for another day, I was still blessed.

Since then, my faith has grown, and I am starting to realize that when everything seems to be going wrong, it is because God is preparing new blessings for me. I just have to trust him, and wait for them. And that is how God works. "Weeping may linger for the night, but joy comes with the morning" (Psalm 30:5).

---

[6] "One Dog Per Verse"

A Short, Sweet Christmas Story

God answers prayers—even when the "wrong" person receives them. Not that there is such a thing as the "wrong" person when it comes to prayer. We need all the prayers we can get.

Christmas is a joyful time for me and my wife. And what is joy, if not to be shared? Every year, I design and print a Christmas card, and because our list is so long, sometimes we end up sending out a card to someone who has moved during the year. That doesn't make our message any less heartfelt. That's exactly what happened at Christmastime, 2006.

This afternoon, just when I was ready to fall flat on my face from exhaustion, the phone rang. The last three days had been real grinders, starting with Sunday morning when our water heater sprung a leak while my wife and I were getting ready to go to church. We had "church" mopping up water in the basement for half the morning, trying to keep ahead of the leak until the serviceman arrived. Monday, we spent half the day waiting for a new water heater to be delivered, and when the man came to install it, he said that it was too difficult to work in such a cramped space and refused to do it. Today, we had another plumber come, and while he was able to install the new water heater, it took all morning and cost twice as much as we had first expected. After getting a great, running jump on preparing for Christmas, our house was a mess and we were really dragging. And then the phone rang.

When I picked up the phone, my caller ID said Claire Spellman, a name I'd never seen before. I figured that it was someone trying to sell me something. When I said "hello," a woman said, "I know you don't know me, but I owe you an apology." As the woman explained, she had opened a Christmas card from us, not noticing it was addressed to the previous tenant in her apartment. She was quite upset about it and told me that she had never met the woman who lived there before her and had no forwarding address for her. I had sent the card to our friend Barbara Hurley, who had booked my gospel quartet, The Gospel Messengers, a couple of times. Barbara had surgery earlier in the fall. I had received an e-mail from her after the surgery, and the last that I knew she was doing all right and was still living at the same address. I assured the woman on the phone that I wasn't upset that she'd inadvertently opened the card, and that I'd most likely be able to get Barbara's mailing address from her church. And then she wanted to talk about the Christmas card.

The front cover of our card looked like a present wrapped with a bow, with the greeting, "Each new day is a gift from God." The woman read the text on the cover to me, saying, "I know all about that!" And then she opened the card and started reading the message on the inside.

And the greatest gift is Jesus Christ
One light to guide us all
One voice to calm all fears
One touch to heal all wounds
One heart to bind all hearts.

She kept telling me how beautiful the card was and how much it meant to her. Then she told me how much she appreciated the note I had written to my friend Barbara. I had written that she was in our hearts and minds and that my wife and I would keep her in prayer. And the woman said, "Oh, I appreciate that so much! I need all the prayers that I can get!" She had accepted the prayers as for her. I told her that I'd seen her name on the caller ID on my phone and thought that she might be related to Deacon Spellman, from our church. She said, "No, we just moved up here from Brooklyn last year. That's probably hard to believe that someone would move up here from Brooklyn." I told her that my wife was from Brooklyn and one of her brothers still lives there, so it didn't sound unbelievable to me.

Finally, when she kept apologizing for mistakenly opening the card, I told her to keep the card as hers. She sounded happy to have it. Sometimes, we can raise the spirits of a complete stranger without even knowing we're doing it. I thanked her for calling me and wished her a very Merry Christmas.

And in lifting her spirits, she lifted mine and my wife's.

A Trip to the Farm

Got sweet heaven in my view hallelujah
*On my journey I press on praise the lord
For I'm bound for that holy city
Got sweet heaven in my view*[7]

The old hymns are filled with visions of being reunited with family and friends after we leave this Earth. Some people envision a heaven where the streets are lined with gold. For others they're the old dirt roads of their childhood.

It's good to touch the green green grass of home[8]

Those who believe that they'll be reunited with family and friends in old familiar places carry a little bit of heaven within them. Not that we have to die to revisit the old homestead or be reunited with family and friends, or even our old beloved dog. They are all there to welcome us in our memories. Sometimes, we step back into those days with a sound or a smell, or an old, familiar song. When we visit our childhood home we are greeted at the door by the memories of those who have gone on before us. It is like a little taste of heaven.

It was a balmy late spring day with clouds scudding their way across the prairie sky and a warm breeze riffling the trees. My wife, Ruth, and I had recently arrived in Janesville on our annual sojourn to celebrate another of Mom's birthdays. This was number ninety-seven. Not that Mom ever limited herself to celebrating her birth

---

[7] "Sweet Heaven in my View"
[8] "Green Green Grass of Home" by Claude Putnam Jr.

"day." It was more like her birth "season." In the week or ten days we'd spend with her, there'd usually be three birthday parties. I'd do a program at Cedar Crest where she lived, and one day we'd drive to New Glarus, a small Swedish village for lunch, always stopping on the way back for a "turtle" sundae at Culver's. Every day would be a special celebration and we would be as heavily scheduled as a small-time politician in October.

On this particular day Mom had a sudden hankering to visit the old Waterman farmstead. It had been a long time since she'd walked the yard and fields there. Not that she was up to doing a lot of walking with her walker. Mom was probably the only living inhabitant of southern Wisconsin who knew the place as the Waterman farm. When she was a little girl, her father rented the farm from Mr. Waterman. Over the years, my Grandpa Holliday had tried his hand at a variety of jobs, like most men of his generation. Whatever it took to put food on the table. For awhile, he was a butcher in the meat department of a grocery store. From there, he moved on to work at Fairbanks Morse in Beloit. In the past, Grandpa'd tried his hand at farming in Black River Falls in northern Wisconsin, and later in Afton, not far down the River Road from Cedar Crest where Mom and Dad would eventually retire. On the Waterman farm, Grandpa Holliday raised cows, pigs, and chickens, and harvested pumpkins, corn, tobacco—whatever there was a market for. With eight kids signed on involuntarily as farm hands, he could afford to diversify. Mom was one step short of being the baby of the family. That role was played by her younger sister, Evelyn, who would grow up to become my Aunt Lynnie. But I am getting ahead of myself. Let me go back for a minute to that early June day when we drove up to the farm.

When Mom decided that she wanted to see the farm, she had no idea it would be for the last time. No one lived in the old wood-framed, paint-peeling, leaning-over-precariously, small gray unassuming house. Our drive up there had been uneventful. The farm was about eight miles from Cedar Crest, two miles short of Milton, where Mom mostly grew up. Driving on the prairie, it might seem at first that there is nothing to see. Most people think that the prairie starts once you cross the Mississippi, but it's "prairie" in southern Wisconsin, sure enough. The prairie sneaks up on you. At first it looks flat and empty. Then you start to feel the gentle roll of the hills. As I described the prairie out in Kansas:

> *I was driving out in Kansas where the land grows flat*
> *Where you wave at the wheat and the wheat waves back*
> *Where the road keeps going just as far as you can see*
> *And I pity any dog that's looking for a tree* [9]

Same prairie, different state.

Laid out over the gently rolling hills is a never-ending geometric pattern of crops. Corn rows gracefully follow the gentle contours of the land, broken only by a small cluster of trees (they're called woods in Wisconsin) and small manmade cow ponds. Coming over the rise of a hill, a whole crazy quilt of farm land unfolds before you: fields of corn, soy beans, tobacco, peas, and rye in the winter to renew the land. But you have to see all of this. It takes more than opening your eyes and looking in the right direction. There's a sound and smell about the prairie that is hard to forget. In late spring, you can still smell the rich, recently plowed fields—the dark fertile soil a gift of the last glaciers that plowed across the area centuries before men first broke the soil with their oxen-pulled plows. Across the fields, you might hear a dog barking or a bell calling the men home to supper. Sound carries a long ways on the prairie.

On the way to the farm, Mom was beginning to rhapsodize about her life there. Those years were special, almost sacred, because her mother was alive back then. As she often said, those were the happiest days of her life. When we reached the farm, we turned into a short driveway leading to the house. The first thing that struck me was how small the house was. For a family of eight children, it must have been cramped. But in the bitter winters when the house was heated by a single potbellied stove, the smallness of the house and rooms must have been a blessing. Standing there, Mom, Ruth, and I saw three different houses. I saw what looked like a lopsided, deserted tenant farm house. And of course, that's what it was. I had no memories to warm me, other than a few old photographs.

Parked next to the house was a pickup truck, but there didn't

---

[9] "Three Speeds Forward and No Speeds Back"

seem to be anyone around. The windows on one side of the house were boarded up and the building pitched precariously toward the driveway. While Ruth and I were seeing our separate houses, Mom was mostly quiet. Maybe she was listening to hear her mother singing in that big farm house kitchen where the family spent so many hours gathered around the kitchen table. Or perhaps she was waiting for her dog Buster to come running down the lane barking a lusty, "Where in the world have you been?" For Mom, the house was haunted with loving memories.

I don't remember how long we stood there, each lost in our own thoughts. Mom walked around a little on her ninety-seven-year-old legs over the uneven dirt of the backyard, broken only by the occasional small clumps of weeds and scraggly grass. There wasn't much to see but everything to remember. There wasn't a lot of talking. It wasn't the kind of thing that needed a lot of words. And then we went back to the car and drove back to Cedar Crest. Mom was tired and lost in memories. For a few minutes she'd had a foretaste of heaven.

Sometimes a Train Is a Train

*T*rains have always held a fascination for musicians. As Paul Simon wrote, "Everybody loves the sound of a train in the distance." Harmonica players coax the sounds of a train starting up at the station, slowly gaining speed, and then rolling on down the tracks with a high-pitched, long whistle. There is no shortage of trains in gospel music either. The titles tell it all: "This Train Is Bound For Glory," "Life's Railway to Heaven," and "There's a Little Black Train a Coming." Where did all of this train imagery in gospel music come from? The explanation is quite simple. In a spoken introduction to a harmonica solo of "This Train," Elder Roma Wilson of Detroit, Michigan, then in his eighties, cleared up any mystery. It says right in the Bible that there was a train pulled up, right in front of the Lord's throne. Isaiah saw it in a vision.

I also saw the Lord sitting upon a throne and his train filled the temple. (Isaiah 6:1)

That was a mighty remarkable vision for Isaiah to see a train, especially back in his day. Unbelievers might say that Isaiah meant a train as a retinue of people. Merriam-Webster defines a train that way. I don't think that would bother old Roma. He'd probably respond with, "If that's the case, how did they get there?"

Visions of heaven are based on a few other references in the Bible. We'll all get crowns of gold when we get there. It says so, more or less, in the Book of Revelation:

And round about the throne were four and twenty seats: and upon the seats I saw four and twenty elders sitting, clothed in white raiment; and they had on their heads crowns of gold. (Revelation 4:4)

If you're going to have a golden crown, I suppose that it naturally follows that you'll get a pair of matching golden slippers.

Singers look with anticipation to the time when they're "going to sit at the Welcome table." Christ offered the invitation: "That ye may eat and drink at my table in my kingdom" (Luke 22:30.

While theologians try to plumb the depths of the imagery in Revelation, just plain folks see heaven much more simply. Sometimes, a train is a train.

When I first started singing in nursing homes, two songs proved to be especially warmly received. The old hymn, "Never Grow Old," had an obvious appeal. A song that I wrote, "Handful of Songs," always touched off a flood of memories, as it talks about the things that we leave behind that are most treasured.

Some may leave money from a lifetime of savings
Some just their name on a marble stone
It's not what you leave, it's the joy of remembering
And all I can leave you is a handful of songs[10]

Occasionally, someone would question how I could sing about death in a nursing home. Death is very real in a nursing home. Facing death alone, marooned in a broken-down body in a lonely nursing home is something that no one would choose as a way to die. But, that's where you're likely to find the Holy Spirit in Industrial Strength.

Some people ask how my wife and I can bear going into nursing homes, because they think that they are so depressing. We find it quite the contrary. The beauty of the faith evidenced in nursing homes is overwhelming at times.

Last week, I sang at a memorial for Ed. Ed was a resident of Gardner Heights Nursing Home for twenty-five years. Even though he had a myriad of serious health problems, he was always there for the monthly service offered up by Reverend Ken Smith, pastor of

---

[10] Handful of Songs"

First Baptist Church in Shelton, Connecticut. He came armed with his Bible and photos of his family, and no matter how much he was suffering, he always had an uplifting word from the Lord. I spent a lot of time in prayer asking the Lord to give me the songs that he wanted me to sing for Ed and all his friends. I thought back to other memorial and funeral services where I'd been asked to sing, and several songs came to mind. When my friend Franklin Cumming's sister-in-law died, his brother asked if the Gospel Messengers would sing at her funeral service. I had just written "When I Get to Glory," and it was one of the songs Frankie wanted us to sing. The song is full of energy, and it was just right for a home-going service.

I don't know about those streets of gold up there
I don't know about them starry crowns
I don't want no golden slippers, Lord
I just want to walk around

CHORUS:
He's going to meet me
Jesus going to meet me there
I'm going to sit down
Sit down in the welcome chair
He's going to greet me
Jesus going to shake my hand
He's going to tell me
Tell me so I'll understand

I'm going to lay down
Lay my heavy burden down
I'll hear the angels
Singing with the sweetest sound
When I get to glory, glory be
What a great day that will be [11]

---

[11] "When I Get to Glory"

There's even a verse with reference to that gospel train:

The train to glory will be coming soon
You know it's time to get on board

The two songs that the Lord put on my heart for Ed's memorial were "Jesus Loves Me," which my mother requested to be sung at her funeral, and a song I'd written recently, "A Sweet, Quiet Peace." "Jesus Loves Me" might seem like an odd choice if all that you've heard is the first verse and the chorus. It's almost always performed by squirmy, itchy-kneed preschoolers in a way that melts the hearts of every grandparent. But, there are two verses that bring great comfort to those who are preparing their hearts and minds for that last, long journey home.

Jesus loves me, loves me still
Though I'm very weak and ill
From his shining throne on high
Comes to watch me where I lie

Jesus loves me, he will stay
Here beside me all the way
If I love him, when I die
He will take me home on high[12]

As the service drew to a close, the Lord led me to sing "A Sweet, Quiet Peace." I had not intended to do it. But the Lord had his own ideas. The song was very fitting, because that is exactly what the Lord gives to those who love him. A dear friend of mine, Allan Antisdel, lived in Maryland. While I never had the chance to meet him in person, I came to know Allan as a man full of grace. He had suffered greatly in his life, but in his final days the Lord blessed him with a peace that transformed his face so dramatically that his wife said that he looked like a young man the day he died. All of the deeply etched lines of suffering were smoothed away. I believe that our friend Ed went home to be with the Lord with the same

---

[12] "Jesus Loves Me" by William B. Bradbury

confidence and peace. My mother knew when she was going. When the train pulled into the station, she had her ticket and was ready to get on board.

I've included the lyrics to "A Sweet, Quiet Peace" as one of the songs in the back of this book. Death awaits us all. For many of us, we have suffering still to face. The chorus of the song offers hope and encouragement.

One thing I know, and this for certain
All will be well, no matter what the future holds[13]

---

[13] "A Sweet, Quiet Peace"

Walking on Water

*W*e like to think that we are in control of our lives. When we wake up in the morning, we set our plans for the day, often forgetting to check with God to see what He has in mind for us. As often as not, our plans start to unravel the moment that our feet hit the floor. One thing after another goes wrong and we find that we're running way behind schedule. When our plan goes out the window, God's plan kicks in.

I had no intentions of writing this. I sat down this morning to write about a checkout line epiphany I had yesterday. After spending a half hour with my concordance seeking scriptural passages that related to that experience with no success, I came across Matthew 14:27–31. At first I thought, "This has nothing to do with yesterday," but I kept rereading the passage. It may not have been relevant to what I'd sat down to write about, but I had the feeling that the Lord had led me to it for a purpose. So I wrote this instead.

I specialize in trying to do things that I have no idea how to do. That's because God has a habit of asking me to do his work without any apparent regard for whether or not I think I can do it. He has a lot more faith in me than I sometimes have in him. But when God asks us to do something, you know that he will give us whatever we need, no matter how impossible the task may seem to be.

In 1977, the Lord asked me to start a gospel quartet. Or, at least I thought that was what he was asking. It seemed like an unreasonable request from my viewpoint. I had just joined the Men's Chorus of Union Baptist Church in Stamford, Connecticut, and it seemed like the height of insensitivity for me to even try to start a gospel quartet within the Chorus. There were so many other members who had sung black gospel most of their lives. At first I thought, "God certainly can't be asking me. I'm a white folk singer from Wisconsin. Perhaps it was a clerical error," but, there's no way to mark "Delivered to Wrong Address, Return to Sender" when the message has come from God. Looking back, I see that I was mostly concerned about what people would think about me, rather than about God. Certainly, he would understand. But the Lord wouldn't let me rest. When he wants you to do something, he doesn't let you off the hook that easily. It wasn't that I couldn't do what God asked me to do. It was that I didn't believe that I could do it.

The Bible is full of stories where people fail to do the Lord's will because of their lack of faith. One of the best remembered is recounted in Matthew:

> Jesus spake unto them saying, Be of good cheer, it is I, be not afraid. And Peter answered him and said Lord if it be thou, bid me come with thee on the water. And he said, come, and when Peter was come down out of the ship, he walked on the water to go to Jesus. But when he saw the wind, boisterous, he was afraid, and beginning to sink, he cried, saying, Lord, save me. And immediately Jesus stretched forth his hand, and caught him and said unto him, Oh thou of little faith, wherefore didst thou doubt. (Matthew 14:27–31)

I see a lot of Peter in me. When God calls me to do something, I start out full of resolve, but when the first stormy billows roll, I become fearful and start to sink. I guess that's what they mean by a "fair-weather friend."

Many years ago I awakened with my heart filled with dread. The previous day I had received an upsetting phone call from a dear friend of mine. He was facing storms in his life that were too much for him to bear, and he couldn't reach out to Jesus because he'd never known him, or God. He couldn't see any way forward, and he was sinking beneath the waves. My heart went out to him because we had shared so much over the years. I'd spoken often about my faith, but it was something that we never shared. Out of compassion and love for him, the words to a song rose up in my heart.

I woke up Monday morning
My heart was filled with pain
Another longtime friend was gone
And he never once blessed your name

And I called out to Jesus:

Jesus, move on the water
Reach out your loving hand
Another poor soul is sinking down
Won't you help him to make a stand[14]

The song was a heartfelt cry to the Lord, and he heard my prayer. After the passing of many years, I still have my friend.

Christ reaches his hand out to us and says, "come." He probably should wear a T-shirt that says, "What part of *come* don't you understand?" Our only response should be, "I'm coming, Jesus!" There are all sorts of reasons why we don't accept his invitation. Some seem very reasonable. Bur Christ has no sympathy for a "Can I get back to you on that?" response. Luke recounts a conversation with three men who expressed their desire to follow after Christ after they'd taken care of earthly business.

And it came to pass when that, as they went in the way a certain man said unto him, Lord, I will follow thee wherever thou goest. And Jesus said unto him, Foxes have holes and birds of the air have nests, but the Son of man hath not where to lay his head. And he said unto another, Follow me, But he said Lord, suffer me first to go and bury my father. Jesus said unto him, Let the dead bury their dead, but go thou and preach the kingdom of God. And another also said, Lord, I will follow thee, but let me first go bid them farewell which are at home at my house. And Jesus said unto him, No man, having put his hand to the plough, and looking back, is fit for the kingdom of God. (Luke 10:57–62)

---

[14] "Jesus, Move on the Water"

When the Lord asks you to do something, don't bother him with questions or excuses. He knows what he is asking, and that you can do it if you will only trust him.

All you got to do is knuckle down to it
Knuckle down, buckle down, do it, do it, do it [15]

The last line of "Jesus, Move on the Water" speaks to our need for unwavering faith.

Jesus walked on the water
Moses parted the sea
You can walk on the water, too
If only you believe

And you can.

---

[15] "You Can't Roller Skate in a Buffalo Herd" by Roger Miller

The Best Laid Plans of Mice and Christians

"Several years ago, my friend Jeanie told me a joke that has stayed with me as one of the most succinct pieces of wisdom I've ever heard. It keeps me in line when I start to get ahead of the Lord: "Want to know how to make God laugh? Tell him your plans for the future."

My wife, Ruth, and I see him every day on the river walk. When we say, "good morning," he makes the slightest of gestures with his hand, smiles, and says something so softly that you wouldn't even know he had spoken if you didn't see his lips moving. He's a short man with black hair peppered with gray and a craggy face, and he walks with a steady, deliberate pace. One morning a few weeks ago when I was out walking by myself, I caught up with him and slowed down to talk for a moment. And then I realized why we never see him talking to anyone. He speaks with a strong Italian accent and speaks haltingly in English. He has just as much trouble understanding English, but as we walked along side by side, we still managed to carry on a conversation.

He spoke modestly about his walking, saying "I can't walk the whole way, but my doctor says that I need to walk for my heart. I walk as far as I can."

"I think that it's great that you walk, "I responded. "I respect anyone who walks, no matter how short a distance. They're doing what they can to take care of their health."

The conversation was brief, because I wanted to walk faster than he could, so I wished him a good day and went on ahead. In the weeks that followed, when my wife and I would pass him on the walk, he'd smile openly and occasionally say "good morning" loud enough so that we could hear him. But up until this morning, I hadn't spoken to him since that first time.

As it turned out, I went for a walk alone today. When I pulled my car in and parked in the lot next to the walkway, I noticed the man getting into his car, which was parked facing mine. He tried to start his car but there was no response, and when he looked up and saw me through his windshield, he smiled broadly. When he got out of the car he tried to tell me that his car wouldn't start. I told him I had some jumper cables in the trunk of my car and pulled around, right next to his car. I hooked up the cables and got into my car, gunning the motor. At first he just stood there smiling until I told him to try to start his car. He smiled and turned his key in the air, turning an imaginary starter and looked at me quizzically. When I said "yes," he got in and gave it a try.

Nothing happened. I got out and asked him if he heard any sound when he turned the key and he just said, "A click." I'm no car mechanic, but I've driven junkers for much of my life, so I know every ailment ever visited on an old car. I asked him to get in and try it once more, but even though I revved my motor while he turned the key, nothing happened. I figured that it was probably the starter.

When we got out of our cars, he handed me his AAA Motor Club card. I asked him if he had a phone and he answered "no." I told him he could use my cell phone, and when he looked uncertainly at me, I offered to call for him. I dialed the number on the card, and after being put on hold for about ten minutes, someone finally came on the line. The woman asked me what the membership number was, which I gave to her, and when she asked my name and address I said, "This isn't my car. I was passing by when I saw that this man was having trouble getting his car started and I just stopped to help him. I'll let you talk to him and he can give you his name and address."

When he had first shown me his AAA Motor Club card, I asked him how he pronounced his last name. His first name is Colagero, which immediately brought to mind the name of the young man in the movie *A Bronx Tale*. I knew how to pronounce his first name because of that movie.

When I asked him how to pronounce his last name (my Italian is fifty years rusty), he spelled it, pointing carefully to each letter on the card. Despite asking him two or three times, he would only spell it. I don't think he understood what I was asking. When the woman on the phone asked his name, he just spelled his last name and gave his address. I had no way of knowing what her next question was, but I could see his confusion. He was having trouble even holding the cell phone so that he could hear her voice, and I had to keep repositioning it for him. He just smiled at her question, turned around and looked hopefully at me, and I offered to speak to the woman. She had a whole string of questions to ask, including the make and year of the car. I could see that it was a Honda Civic and asked him, "What year is the car?" and he answered, "2000."

"What is the problem?" she asked.

"I'm pretty sure that it's the starter," I said. "I had the starter go on the car I'm driving in this same parking lot a couple of years ago."

Then she asked me, "Where does he want the car towed to?" and I asked her, "Can they tow it to the gas station closest to his house, and have someone give him a ride home while it's being repaired? And she said, "He's a platinum card member and he can have the car towed up to one hundred miles."

"He lives in Ansonia, and I'm looking across the parking lot at the town, so it shouldn't be that long a tow," I answered. I didn't want to leave him stranded at the gas station. When I asked her how long it would take for the tow truck to get there, she said, "No longer than an hour and a half."

"An hour and a half? I could push the car home in that amount of time!"

She assured me that that was the longest it would take. Because he didn't have a phone for them to call him back, she said it was important that he stay by his car and keep an eye out for the tow truck. That's a long time to keep your eye out.

When we'd finished our conversation, she said, "It was nice of you to help the man out," and I answered, "I'm just glad that I happened by."

After I got off the phone, I tried to explain to him everything she had said. I'm not sure he understood what I said other than he was going to have a long wait. I offered to walk over to a McDonald's across the street and bring him back a cup of coffee and an Egg McMuffin, or whatever he wanted, but he told me that he'd already eaten before he came. I hated to see him just standing there by the car for all that time.

As I prepared to head off for my walk, he kept thanking me profusely. I threw my arms around him and gave him a hug and said, "God Bless you. The Lord brought me here so that you'd have someone to help you."

In all the times we've seen the man walking, we've never once seen him talking to someone. It may be because he has difficulty speaking English. I thought back to that time a few weeks ago when I walked alongside him, and realized that I might be the only person he knows on the walkway. Even though English is a little awkward for him, and my college Italian is only dimly remembered, we were able to communicate through hand gestures, facial expressions, smiles, and laughter. We spoke more fluently with our eyes than with our tongues. Earlier, when I looked into his car as he was trying to start the motor, I noticed he had a thin silver chain with a cross hanging from his rearview mirror. He was traveling in good company. I felt that Christ was there with us, helping us to communicate despite the language barrier between us. After all, Christ promised, "For where two or three are gathered together in my name, there am I in the midst of them" (Matthew 18:20).

Christ knows no barriers.

When I started out this morning, Colagero was not in my plans. I didn't even know his name. I was running an hour behind my schedule, but I was right on God's time.

A Footnote

This morning, I went for a walk alone again. My wife was still not quite over the cold she caught last week. I went armed with a few phrases in Italian, sent to me by a friend, hoping to see Colagero. He was no where to be seen, but as I was walking along, I saw another river walk regular. He's about Colagero's size, but looks considerably older. Like Colagero, he never speaks, but he always has a warm smile for me, even though he never answers my greeting of "good morning." Sometimes he just reaches out his hand toward me as I am passing, and I reach over and touch his sleeve. He's there every day and does the full three-and-a-half miles, six inches at a time. It must take him ten thousands steps to cover the full length of the walk. When I passed him this morning I said, "Good Morning! Buon Giorno!" and "Buenos Dias!" He smiled broadly, tipped his cap, and said, "Buenos Dias!" I figured that about covered it. That was our whole conversation. It was enough.

A Final Footnote

This morning, once again, I headed off alone for my walk, hoping to see Colagero. Sure enough, I wasn't more than a few hundred yards down the walkway when I caught up to him. As I approached him, I called out cheerfully, "Buon Giorno, Calagero, Come sta?" And he answered "Good morning." The next time I see him, I'm going to say "Guten morgen!"

Oh, and by the way, it *was* the starter . . .

Story Listeners

*L*istening is a gift that not everyone has. It requires stepping out of ourselves and into the life of someone else. Any urge to judge has to be set aside. When people need to talk, more often than not, it's not because they are seeking advice. Don't offer any, unless it is asked for. They just need to feel that someone understands them. In a way, it's not that important that you do. It just means a lot to them that you care enough to stop and listen. And who knows—maybe you'll learn something.

Everyone has a story to tell: a lifetime of stories. Stories are different than anecdotes. Anecdotes usually start out with, "That reminds me of the time . . ." Anecdotes tell about something that happened. Stories come from the heart. And every story requires a listener.

In *The Heart Is a Lonely Hunter*, Mr. Singer, who is a deaf-mute, lives a life of isolation, his stories buried inside of him. The only person he could "talk" to was his deaf-mute friend who was a child living in a man's body. But Mr. Singer was a story listener. He could read lips and he listened with rapt attention. Those who poured out their dreams and frustrations to him felt he cared about them in a way that no one else did. His compassion shone through, and they somehow knew that no matter how intimate a secret they shared with him, he would not judge them. But the best story listener was Jesus. No person was so lowly or unacceptable to others that Christ wouldn't open his heart to them.

Publicans, harlots, beggars and thieves
Jesus was a friend to them all
He ate at their tables and walked on their streets
And he comforted their weary souls[16]

You never know when Christ will send someone to you, who needs to talk with you:

If you meet a stranger, welcome him in
Don't leave him standing at your door
You can never tell who Jesus will send
Whether they are rich or poor

Several years ago, I was walking across the parking lot of a Grand Union supermarket. It was a beautiful, sunny day and I had a bounce in my step when I heard a car horn blowing. I looked around to see where it was coming from, and saw a woman parked at the edge of the lot with her window rolled down, waving to me. I turned and walked over to the car, figuring that it was someone I knew. When I got close enough, I realized I had never seen her before. When I got up to the car, she said "Hello, I wanted to ask you to pray for my mother."

She had a story to tell. I stood there, leaning against the side of her car and she poured her heart out. Her mother was in the hospital and she was very concerned for her. I asked her mother's name and told her that not only would I pray for her, but that my wife and I would visit her in the hospital. I asked her why she thought that I would pray for her mother, and she said, "When I saw you walking across the parking lot, you looked like a minister." I told her that I wasn't, but she understood her needs better than I did. She needed someone to minister to her and somehow she sensed I would. We are all ministers, and you never can tell who Jesus will send to you for ministering.

People seek out story listeners wherever they can find them. Supermarkets seem to be as good a place as any. More recently, I stopped at a Big Y on the way home to pick up a couple of items. I

---

[16] "Didn't My Jesus Die For All?" by Jerry Rasmussen

was standing in the Express Checkout line when I glanced back, and out of the corner of my eye saw a woman standing behind me. I made room on the conveyor belt and invited her to put her groceries down before noticing that all she was buying was a small greeting card. I smiled when I saw that and said, "I'd hate to have you standing in line holding that heavy card," and she laughed. And the floodgates opened. She told me that it was a thank-you card for her brother. She said, "He just bought me a new Chevrolet Suburban SUV and paid for my insurance, and I wanted to let him know how much I appreciate it." I said that she must have a wonderful brother, and she started talking about how she washes his clothes and cleans his house, and all the things that she does for him. I responded by saying "When you do something good for someone else, you'll get your reward when you least expect it." She needed to talk to someone. It just happened to be me. As I left, I told her to have a good day and to enjoy her car.

Sometimes a casual conversation can unexpectedly open up into an honest discussion of faith. A few weeks ago, I was at my podiatrist's for a checkup. Caring for someone's feet is a holy profession. After all, Jesus washed the apostles' feet and told them that they should do the same for others.

Ye call me Master and Lord; and ye say well; for so I am. If I then, your Lord and Master, have washed your feet; ye also ought to wash one another's feet. (John 13:13–14)

I'm not sure how the conversation wandered on to miracles, but it was something that my podiatrist wanted to talk about. He asked me if I believed in miracles. I told him that I did, and that I didn't see any reason why miracles should have stopped after Christ's lifetime. He goes into private homes to care for elderly, home-bound patients and talked with emotion of a particular woman whose bedroom is like a shrine, filled with religious figures, pictures, and several burning votive candles. My podiatrist could understand how miracles happen to someone of such great faith, but he asked, "Why do miracles happen to people who aren't even very religious?" I thought of Paul on the road to Damascus being blinded by the light of Jesus Christ who appeared before him. Paul certainly was a "very religious" Jew, but he was persecuting the Christians. My answer to my podiatrist's question was, "Maybe it's the people who don't believe who are the most in need of a miracle. God has certainly used great sinners to do his will. If you had to be 'religious' to be used by the Lord, his work would never get done."

We had a wonderful conversation, as unexpected as it was enjoyable. It would never have happened if I hadn't taken the time to listen.

There's a wonderful line in a song by Carmen McRae:

Never stopped to listen,
Never missed a chance to speak[17]

There are people all around us whose hearts are lonely hunters. They have a hunger to share their stories with someone who is compassionate and understanding. Don't turn them from your door. Take the time to listen to them, to encourage them, and to pray for them. Christ would do no less. Better yet, tell them about Jesus. No one listens as lovingly and with as much compassion as Christ.

---

[17] "Livin' " by T. Garvin

A Mustard Seed

*W*hen you've got a good thing, you want to tell other *people about it. That's what's called "word of mouth" advertising. And there's nothing as good as Jesus. The beautiful thing is that Jesus is there for the asking. It may take a lifetime of prayer before a friend or loved one finally opens their heart to Christ and welcomes him in. It's worth the wait.*

Once in a while, we are blessed to share in the excitement when someone welcomes Christ into their lives. It's an experience we'll never forget.

My brother-in-law Everett called me this morning, his voice filled with excitement. Over the last few months, I've been sending him the writings for this book, a batch at a time. Everett lives in a Senior Housing apartment complex and has enjoyed sharing the writings with his friends there. I gave him the most recent copies earlier this week, and as always, he brought them down to the lounge to read. While he was sitting there reading, a woman spotted him and came over to ask him what he was reading. When he told her, she asked if he would let her read them, too. Everett handed some of the pages to her and she sat there with him, quietly reading. When she finished, she told Everett that she was so inspired, she "felt like Superman." Later that day, she was passing a church, and when she noticed it was open, she was drawn to go in. She didn't know what denomination the church was, but that wasn't important to her. As it turned out, it was a Catholic church, and while she was there, she met a priest to whom she spoke at some length. As she told Everett, she couldn't remember the last time she'd been in a church. It was thirty or forty years ago.

Last night, the woman stopped in the lounge again and saw

Everett sitting there. She wanted to talk. One of the writings that had moved her so much was the one about "Story Listeners." She recognized Everett as a "story listener," and she had a story to tell. For the next three hours she talked to him, pouring out her life story. She said she was so inspired by the writings that she wanted to know if he would loan them to her so she could make copies to send to her daughter. And then she said she wanted to go to church with Everett on Sunday. After all those years, she felt called to go back to worship. She asked him if he had an extra Bible she could read, and when he told her that he didn't, she said she would go out and buy one. She was willing to spend as much as fifty dollars. Everett told her of a bookstore in the area, and she went off to get the first Bible she'd had in many years.

Everett and I marveled at what God can do with even the smallest act of faith. Christ, in talking about the Kingdom of God, spoke this parable about faith:

It is like a grain of mustard seed, which when it is sown in the earth, is less than all the seeds that be in the earth. But when it is sown, it groweth up, and becometh greater than all herbs, and shooteth out great branches; so that the fowls of the air may lodge under the shadow of it. (Mark 4:31–32)

Many years ago, I wrote a song with a similar imagery of a seed:

Share the water, plant the seed
All who hunger to be freed
And all who ask shall be released
Love is the beginning[18]

Every loving act that we do in the name of Jesus, no matter how small, is a mustard seed. More often than not, we are not privileged to see the seed grow into a great tree. It is not our job to see the results, just to plant the seed. But, once in awhile, God shows us the fruits of our modest labors. He does it as an encouragement to us. A small seed was planted in my heart when I wrote the pages that I sent

---

[18] "Pebble, Wheel, and Seed"

to Everett. He in turn planted the seed in the woman and a small shoot appeared out of the ground. As the seed grows in her, she will plant new seeds in those she meets. And the angels in heaven rejoiced, this day.

Another sheep returned to the fold.

Abiding

*J*esus is God's right-hand man. As they say, "It's not what you know, it's who you know." If there ever was someone you ought to know, it's Jesus. All good things flow from him.

I am the vine, ye are the branches: He that abideth in me, and I in him, the same bringeth forth much fruit; for without me ye can do nothing. (John 15:5)

Bruce Wilkerson wrote a transforming book just on that passage in scripture titled *Secrets of the Vine*. It's a small book that has had a large impact on my life. Who could refuse such a generous offer from our Lord? And yet, we often do. At the heart of the matter, I believe, is that we are not willing to surrender completely to Jesus. There are old habits and destructive patterns in our lives that we are not willing to relinquish. At least that's been a problem for me. You have to surrender complete control of your life to Jesus. Not just part of it. You can't abide in Christ just when you get in trouble. He's not going to stick around if he is just your spiritual Band-Aid. If you don't give yourself completely to Christ, that's where the second half of the sentence kicks in: "without me, ye can do nothing." We all know the truth of that.

"Abide in me" is an invitation into an intimate relationship with Christ. There is leisureliness in abiding in Christ. He reveals himself to us at his own pace. If we are to abide in Christ, we must set aside all the daily distractions of our lives so that we can luxuriate in the pleasure of his company. It is in the quietness of abiding that we fully come to know Jesus. There is prayer in abiding, and time spent in the Word, but just as importantly, there is listening. Just as Brer' Rabbit had his special "Laughing Place," each of us has our own

"Abiding Place." It may be a special chair or room. Walking in the garden, whatever your "garden" is, may be your Abiding Place. As it says in Ecclesiastes: "To every thing there is a season, and a time to every purpose under heaven" (Ecclesiastes 3:1).

Your time may be at night:

As I lie here on my bed at night
Tossing and turning, Lord what shall I do?
I pray to Jesus, lead me to the light
May I abide in you[19]

When Jesus wants to talk with you in the dead of the night, don't worry about not getting your rest. There is nothing as restful as abiding in the Lord. He will renew your strength and heal your weary body.

Abiding in Christ isn't just a darkened-room experience, though. When we learn to completely trust in the Lord, we carry him in our heart throughout our days. We may not always be aware of Christ's presence, but there are times when he reveals himself to us. It is in those times when we see most clearly, because we see through the eyes of Christ.

Oswald Chambers, in his book *My Utmost for His Highest* talks about salvation in the same terms that I use for abiding. He says it much better than I do: "The salvation that comes from God means being completely delivered from myself, and being placed into perfect union with Him. Salvation means . . . that the Spirit of God has brought me into intimate contact with the true person of God himself."

When we abide completely in Christ, our life is transformed. We may not always be conscious of the transformation, but others can see it in us. As the apostle John wrote: "He that saith he abideth in him ought to himself so to walk, even as he walked" (1 John: 2:6).

Ultimately, Christ's promise to abide in us holds the greatest of rewards. Paul tells us:

---

[19] "May I Abide in You" by Jerry Rasmussen

60

"The fruit of the Spirit is love, joy, peace, long-suffering, gentleness, goodness, faith" (Galatians 5:22).

Abiding in Christ gives us comfort and healing. It gives us understanding and courage. It fills our hearts with the Holy Spirit. Armed with these gifts, we can boldly step forward into the world. Our works will bring glory to God because they arise from the intimacy of abiding in Christ.

A Train Story

Maybe it's because people are traveling and they don't expect to ever see their fellow passengers again. I've had several experiences where a total stranger sat down next to me and poured out their heart. In most instances, I didn't know the person's name and I never heard from them again. Just like the little girl singing "A Mighty Fortress Is Our God" for me when I was struggling, the Lord has used me to help others. He uses all of us. God knows "we're no angels." But sometimes God gives us their work to do.

Here's another traveling story, this time when my wife and I were coming back to Connecticut after we'd taken a trip out west.

He got on in Chicago. He was a striking figure . . . not because he was unusually tall, muscular, or handsome. When he came down the aisle, he was carrying a bedroll on his shoulder (something you wouldn't expect to see on a train going to New York City). He was wearing work jeans, a cowboy hat, boots, and a T-shirt. Nothing unusual for him, as it turned out, but very out of sync with everyone else on the train. I noticed the T-shirt right away because it had a drawing of an old battle-scarred White-faced steer with one broken horn. The saying on the back was "Does Not Play Well with Others." I got a big kick out of that.

I'd guess he was in his late forties or early fifties by the deep lines around the corners of his eyes. He looked like he spent a lot of his time outdoors, and as it turned out, that was exactly the case. He made a living as a hunting guide, taking Easterners out to shoot elk and moose in the Grand Tetons. No wonder he looked so out of place in a Pullman car heading for New York City: Moose Dundee. It took many hours for his story to slowly unfold. He was on his way to New

York City to try to convince the woman he loved to come back out to Wyoming with him. He'd driven his truck from the Tetons to Iowa, and took a bus or train to Chicago. He didn't say which. He said that he really hated to go to New York City, but it would be worth it if he could talk the woman into coming back with him. She'd come out and lived with him in the Grand Tetons for a few weeks but hated it. He said it drove her nuts to have to drive so far to go shopping. Never underestimate the importance of shopping. I can understand her, though. In Wyoming, you may have to drive forty or fifty miles to the next big town . . . a town of two to three thousand people. We went though one town with a population of ten, so the towns that were several hundred seemed like real metropolises.

As his story unfolded, I thought of my father and a song I'd written about him. When my father was in his early twenties, he drove all the way from Wisconsin to Montana in his new model T Ford, picking up work in the fields along the way, to try to convince the woman he loved to come back with him. She had moved out there, right at the flash point of their romance, and like the man coming to New York City, my father thought that it was worth the trip just to try to bring her back. As the song says, "Love can bloom, even out in Montana." My father didn't succeed, which was good for me, because he later met the woman he married who was my mother. Some of the verses to the song kept playing in my head as the man talked:

> It's a hell of a drive just to say "Hello"
> And "How are you doing" and "I miss you so"
> And "Why did you have to move so far away?"
> Why'd you move all the way to Montana[20]

After my father got out to Montana and was standing there at her door, it was clear to him that the trip was all in vain:

> With his hands in his pocket and his shirt tail out
> He could tell in a moment that the fire'd gone out
> And there's no sense in mooning like a love-sick fool
> Who would drive all the way to Montana

---

[20] "Montana"

I hoped that my Wyoming friend wouldn't have the same reception.

As we were heading in to New York, I pointed out the Hudson River to the man, and then the George Washington Bridge. He became very quiet, finally, and we were all trying to get our luggage together, so we didn't have a chance to say a final good- bye. But I wished him well. In a way, he was in a win-win situation. If the woman decided she loved him enough to go back with him and make a good life in Wyoming, I hoped that everything would work out for them. It's hard to make a true connection with someone, and it's well worth doing whatever it takes to hold on to them. If she refused to go back with him, in the long run that may have been good, too. He had to know. No sense regretting that you never tried.

The Gate of Beautiful

I always find it interesting that people who are offended when you talk about faith and insist that they don't live their life on faith, do just that. They can deny it until the White-faced steers come home. You can't live without faith. You can live without believing in God—if you call that living.

We are of limited vision. Even those with the strongest faith cannot completely grasp the breadth and depth of God's power. When we come to God in prayer, we have to leave our childish vision behind and ask God to bless us in his infinite love and mercy. Nobody beats God's giving.

Sometimes we don't ask for enough. God's power is limitless, and yet we limit him. When my son Aaron first struck out on his own, I offered some good advice. "Don't let anyone else define you," and "Don't limit who you can be." Like all good advice, I try to take it with breakfast, every morning. It's something we need to constantly remind ourselves of. "That's not who I am." There's another self-imposed limit. For Christians, it's not a matter of who I am, but who God wants me to be. Life is an endless "becoming." Thank God that he sees our potential, and often blesses us far beyond our most fervent prayers.

There is a wonderful story in the Bible about a miraculous healing performed by the apostle Peter.

Now Peter and John went up together into the temple at the hour of prayer, being the ninth hour. And a certain man, lame from his mother's womb was carried, whom they laid at the gate of the temple which is called Beautiful, to ask for alms of them that entered the temple; who seeing Peter and John about to go into the temple asked for an alms. And Peter, fastening his eyes upon him with John, said, Look on us. And he gave heed unto them, expecting to receive something of them. Then Peter said, Silver and gold have I none; but such as I have give I thee; In the name of Jesus Christ of Nazareth rise up and walk. And he took him by the right hand, and lifted him up; and immediately his feet and ankle bones received strength. (Acts 3:1–7)

The man got much more than he bargained for. God is that way.

It's understandable that the man at the gate of Beautiful set his sights so low. For him, it was a reasonable request. After all, he'd been crippled from birth. Long ago, he had accepted who he was. That can be a good thing. Before we can become who we were created to be, we have to accept who we are. Then with God's grace, we start becoming. Every day, we sit at the gate of Beautiful. As we approach God, too often we set limits on what we ask him to do. God has prepared blessings far greater than any we can imagine.

Many years ago I was told a wonderful story. A man had just died and gone to heaven. He had lived a righteous life, and God had blessed him bounteously. As Saint Peter was showing him around the streets of heaven, he pointed out all the beautiful buildings and talked about the wonders they held. When they were passing a particularly large building, Peter remained strangely silent. It seemed like he was in a hurry to get past it. Sensing Peter's reluctance to talk about the building, the man asked him, "What is in that building?" and Peter answered, "You don't want to know." Of course, that only aroused the man's curiosity and he started pestering Peter: "Please show me what is in the building!" Finally, Peter relented and said, "I'll show you, but you'll wish that I hadn't."

When they entered the building they looked at seemingly endless rows of shelving that rose from floor to ceiling. The shelves were filled with box after box. When the man asked, "What is in the boxes?" Peter told him, "The boxes are filled with blessings that God prepared for you that you never asked for." And the man was heartbroken. The word "limit" is used in the Bible one time. The word "love" appears 306 times. That should tell you something about God. When you stand at the gate of Beautiful, trust in God's love and he will shower you with bountiful blessings far greater than any your mind could ever imagine.

The Eyes of Faith

*F*or me, songwriting, letter writing, and even Christmas card writing flows together naturally. A simple phrase may elicit a long letter, which can evolve into a song, and then become a message on a Christmas card. I ended up writing a song, "May My Heart Find Rest in Thee" that grew out of this writing, and lines from the song became the message in a Christmas card.

It's one of those phrases that comes at you sideways. You're listening to someone talking and suddenly it hits you. This was one of those occasions. Reverend Dennis Albrecht was preaching a sermon at St. John's Lutheran Church when he used the phrase, "The eyes of faith." In the following weeks as I reflected on that statement, I realized how differently we perceive the world around us when we have a strong faith. No wonder it is so difficult to discuss religion with those who do not believe in God. We see things so differently. "Blessed are the eyes which see the things that ye see" (Luke 10:23).

Christ often spoke in parables that made no sense to those who did not believe. "Therefore speak I to them in parables; because they seeing see not; and hearing they hear not, neither do they understand" (Matthew 13:13).

Christ is talking about much more than mere vision. We can read a passage in the Bible a hundred times before its meaning suddenly becomes clear to us. Revelation comes slowly, even to the most faithful. In the same way, we walk through our lives as if we were sleepwalking. Our minds are a thousand miles away. We could pass Christ on the street, and not even notice.

If Jesus should come back, just for a day
And preach on that corner to all who pass by
Who'd stop and listen, and who'd walk away?
And turn from salvation, and never know why?[21]

In the Sermon on the Mount, Christ spoke of the righteous that had helped someone who was in need. They did not understand that, in helping someone, they were doing it to Jesus.

"Then shall the righteous answer him, saying, 'Lord, when saw we thee ahungered, and fed thee? or thirsty, and gave thee drink? When saw we thee a stranger, and took thee in? Or naked, and clothed thee? Or when saw we thee sick, or in prison and came to thee?' " In responding to their confusion, Christ said: "And the King shall say unto them, 'Verily I say unto you, Inasmuch as ye have done it unto one of the least of these my brethren, ye have done it unto me' " (Matthew 25:37–40).

To those who turned a blind eye to someone in need, Christ said:

"For I was ahungered, and ye gave me no meat; I was thirsty, and ye gave me no drink. I was a stranger, and ye took me not in; naked, and ye clothed me not; sick, and in prison and ye visited me not" (Matthew 25:42–43).

How wonderful it would be if we could see Christ in others. We would treat each other with the love and compassion of Christ, rather than walk in darkness.

And in the darkness, give me the eyes of faith.[22] Seeing is more than just looking at something. It is absorbing what you see so that you understand it and it becomes a part of you. In *The Little Prince,* by Antoine De Saint Exupery, there is a wonderful conversation that the Little Prince has with a fox. When they first met, they had approached each other very warily. It took several meetings and conversations before they became friends and came to love each other. When it came time for the fox to leave, he spoke these words of wisdom:

---

[21] "Last Chance for Salvation" by Jerry Rasmussen
[22] "May My Heart Find Rest in Thee" by Jerry Rasmussen

"Good-bye," said the fox. "Here is my secret: it's quite simple. One sees clearly only with the heart. Anything essential is invisible to the eyes."

When you accept Christ into your heart, it is as if a veil is removed from your eyes and a whole new world opens before you.

I once was blind, but now I see.[23]

---

[23]"Amazing Grace" by John Newton

Bet Hedgers

*I*t no longer surprises me when friends who profess that they don't believe there is a God ask me to pray for them when they are facing a serious illness. It's happened so many times. These are the same people who claim to be too logical to believe in something that can't be proven. They claim that they don't take anything on "faith" and will argue vehemently if you say that not everything they believe can be proven. They're not even particularly fond of the word "believe." I believe that everyone puts their faith in something, whether it's the human mind or a supreme being. It's just a matter of who you trust with your life: yourself, or God.

Even atheists and agnostics sometimes hedge their bets. I've heard people who insist they don't believe in God add, "But, if there is a God, he'll still let me in to heaven because I try to live a good life." Then there are the people who claim there is no God, but who want you to pray for them, just in case there is. If people don't believe in heaven, they still think that they should be able to go there. Many years ago, I was at a folk festival and sang a song that I'd just written. These are a couple of the verses:

Publicans, harlots, beggars, and thieves
Jesus was a friend to them all
He ate at their tables and walked on their streets
And he comforted their weary souls

Lutherans, Baptists, Catholics, and Jews
Whether they are black or white

Buddhists and Muslims, Methodists, too
All are precious in his sight[24]

(I was a Methodist at the time, so I could kid around about it.)

After the song, a man came up, obviously upset with me. He said, "Why didn't you include atheists?" I asked him "Why would you care whether you're included in a song about the son of God, if you don't believe in God? Have you ever tried to come up with a rhyme for atheist?" He didn't have an answer to either question. He didn't believe there was a God, but he didn't want to be left out. I think the message of the song is true. Christ wasn't crucified just for Christians. He was crucified for mankind. The one thing that all the faiths mentioned in the song have in common is they all believe in God. The man was right in asking, though. I believe God does love atheists and agnostics and that they are precious in his sight. Just because they don't believe he exists doesn't mean he doesn't love them. The disgruntled man was trying to hedge his bet. He wanted it both ways. Fence-sitting may work in politics, but it doesn't when it comes to faith. Christ is very clear about that. And being "good" isn't a ticket to heaven. When it comes to being "good," even the best of us fall short of the mark. Luke recounts a conversation between Christ and a young ruler that gets right to the point:

And a certain ruler asked him saying, Good Master, what shall I do to inherit eternal life? And Jesus said unto him, Why callest thou me good? None is good, save one, that is, God. (Luke 18:18–19)

If Christ doesn't feel worthy to be called good, how can we?

The whole concept of a side door for unbelievers who've tried to live a good life may be comforting, but it certainly is not what Christ taught. When he was asked what was the greatest commandment, Christ said: "Thou shalt love the Lord thy God with all thy heart, and with all thy soul and with all thy mind" (Matthew 22:37). And as Christ said, "If you love me, keep my commandments" (John 4:15).

Back when I was in college, I had a roommate who had his own

---

[24] "Didn't My Jesus Die for All?"

take on salvation. He was very straightforward about it. He said that he was going to have a good time and take every pleasure he could in his life, whether it was a sin or not. He figured that if God was all merciful, then he could repent at the last minute, like the thief who hung on a cross beside Jesus. My roommate had an Exit Strategy. I don't think it works that way. It's not what you say on your dying bed—it's the state of your soul.

Our salvation didn't come cheaply. It was paid at the greatest of all prices: the crucifixion of Christ on the cross. To think that we can cruise through life, doing whatever we please, and then expect Christ to rescue us like the U.S. Cavalry, is downright blasphemous. While we can't earn our salvation through our good works, God expects us to put him first in our lives.

No matter what they tell you, there's no free lunch
No guaranteed money in the bank
You can't get to heaven in an easy chair
You've got to give it everything it takes.[25]

A life spent serving ourselves is a life wasted. Our very life is a gift, and it can be taken away at a moment's notice. Loving God isn't primarily an emotional activity. Our love is reflected in the way we live, and each day offers many opportunities to serve God, no matter how menial the task may be. At the end of the day, we should ask ourselves the question:

Have I given anything, today?
Have I helped some needy soul on my way
When I come to take my rest, just to know I've done my best
And my name, my name, my name be written there today[26]

Sooner or later, conversations with people who don't believe in God come down to one thing. Can people who don't believe in God go to heaven? That's a very difficult subject. We all have loved ones who don't believe, and it is very painful to think that they will not be

---

[25] "Drowning in the Details of Life" by Jerry Rasmussen
[26] "Help for the Needy" by Thomas A. Dorsey

saved. We pray for them, but we have no power of our own to change their hearts. When I'm asked that question, my answer may sound flippant and evasive. I say, "Why are you asking me? I'm not in charge of admissions." There is a lot of truth in that. It's not up to me, who gets into heaven and who doesn't make the final cut. But again, Christ was very clear:

> Verily, verily, I say unto thee, except a man be born again he cannot see the kingdom of God. (John 3:3)

You'll notice that he didn't say, "Except a man *say* that he is born again." Not all who say that they have been "born again" have been. Christ spoke out strongly against those who call on his name but do not serve him:

> Not every one that saith unto me, Lord, Lord, shall enter into the kingdom of heaven; but he that doeth the will of my Father, which is in heaven. Many will say to me in that day, "Lord, Lord, have we not prophesied in thy name? And then will I profess unto them, I never knew you; depart from me, ye that work iniquity. (Matthew 7:21–23)

There's an old song that asks "Which Side Are You On?" There are no fences in that question. And no hedges, either. It is up to each of us to make our own personal commitment to Jesus Christ.

Cross Purposes

*T*here was a time when the cross was honored with the
greatest reverence. The old hymns sing its praises:

So I'll cherish that old rugged cross
till my trophies at last I lay down
I will cling to the old rugged cross
And exchange it someday for a crown[27]

The top of every steeple in the country proudly displayed the
cross as a reminder of the price Christ paid for our sins, and the
victory he won for us by his death. We were taught that our salvation
came through the cross. These are hard times for the cross. It has
become an accessory to wear, with no thought of its holiness. You
see Rap and Hip-Hop singers in the music videos on television,
gyrating and spouting obscenities, with heavy chains around their
necks that are adorned with a cross. In some of the largest
contemporary churches, a cross is nowhere to be found. The
emphasis is on having an upbeat, joyful worship experience, and the
cross is dismissed as a symbol of death, not redemption. Nobody
wants to think about Christ suffering on the cross, when they're
having a good time.

When I read of Christ's life, I am constantly struck by its
simplicity. By our standards, he lived a life of modest comforts.
Throughout the three years of his ministry, Christ was constantly on
the road. What he owned, he carried on his back. Jesus, in speaking
to a scribe who expressed a desire to follow him, said:

---

[27] "The Old Rugged Cross" by George Bennard

The foxes have holes, and the birds of the air have nests, but the Son of man hath not where to lay his head. (Matthew 8:20)

Christ never offered comfort to those who chose to follow him. He offered a cross to bear:

And he said to them all, "if any man will come after me, let him deny himself, and take up his cross daily, and follow me. For whosoever will save his life shall lose it; but whosoever will lose his life for my sake, the same shall save it. For what is a man advantaged, if he gain the whole world, and lose himself, and be cast away?" (Luke 9:23–25)

Following Jesus was never meant to be a "walk in the park." "Narrow is the way, which leadeth unto life, and few there be that find it." (Matthew 7:14).

The symbol of Christianity is a cross, not an easy chair. As for material goods, Christ made it clear where our priorities must be. In speaking with a rich young ruler who asked him, "What shall I do to inherit eternal life?" Christ said to him, "although you have kept the commandments:

Yet lackest thou one thing; sell all that thou hast, and distribute unto the poor, and thou shalt have treasure in heaven; and come follow me.' And when he heard this, he was very sorrowful" (Luke 18:22–23).

Those who followed Jesus were blessed with great riches, but those riches were not material. They were riches of the Spirit. Their blessings came from their obedience, self-denial, and humility. Like Jesus, they suffered indignities and abuse of the worst kind, sometimes ending up by being crucified, as Peter was. It was a hard, holy life. The apostles had very little, and yet they had everything they needed.

There is much being made of the revival in Christianity in this country. Thousands flock to megachurches, and the television channels are bursting with ministries in preaching and singing. One of the most financially successful forms of worship is teaching what is referred to as the "Prosperity Gospel," a belief that wealth and power are rewards for pious Christians. A particularly influential early practitioner of this style of preaching was Rev. Kenneth Hagin, a Word of Faith minister. He thought that the problem with Christianity was that the church was focused on the cross. As he stated, "The trouble with us is that we've preached a 'cross' religion . . . the cross is actually a place of death, and you leave people in death." There is a reason why the cross has been such a powerful symbol of salvation. The cross was a place of victory over death. The old hymn, "Near the Cross," beautifully expresses a very different attitude than that of Reverend Hagin:

Jesus keep me near the cross – There's a precious fountain
Free to all a healing stream, Flows from Calvary's mountain

CHORUS:
In the cross, in the cross be my glory ever
Till my raptured soul shall find Rest, beyond the river[28]

The most successful preacher of the Prosperity Gospel today is Joel Osteen, whose congregation is the largest in the country. There are no crosses prominently displayed in his church because he preaches a very upbeat Christianity. When he was interviewed by Larry King, he was asked the question: "Is it hard to lead a Christian life?" Osteen responded, "I don't think it's that hard; to me, it's fun." Paul's letter to the Galatians presented a very different picture of the Christian life: "For every man shall bear his own burden" (Galatians 6:5).

Osteen believes that, as a child of God, we can receive "preferential treatment." He bases this belief on the scriptural passage: "A good man obtaineth favor of the Lord, but a man of wicked devices will he condemn" (Proverbs 12:2). His book, *Your Best Life Now,* refers to several other scriptural passages that speak of God bestowing his favor on those who serve him. In example after example, Osteen states how God blesses Christians financially, or with material gifts. It is an appealing message. By claiming the

---

[28] "Near the Cross" by William H. Doanne

Lord's favor, we can obtain job promotions, parking spaces, and preferred seating. Osteen says that all that is necessary is to wake up declaring you have God's favor.

What does Jesus say about how we should live as Christians? Christ spoke of serving others, not seeking preferential treatment for yourself:

> Even as the Son of man came not to be ministered unto, but to minister and give his life as a ransom for many. (Matthew 21:27)

As evidence of Jesus' humility, he washed the apostles' feet. When Peter protested, Christ said to him, "Ye call me Master and Lord; and ye say well; for so I am. If I then your Lord and Master have washed your feet; ye also ought to wash one another's feet" (John 13:13–14).

Jesus had something to say about priority seating, too:

> When thou art bidden of any man to a wedding, sit not down in the highest room, lest a more honorable man than thou be bidden of him . . . . For whosoever exalteth himself shall be abased, and he that humbleth himself shall be exalted. (Luke 14:8, 11)

Preachers of the Prosperity Gospel believe that pious Christians have a right to financial wealth as well. Reverend Charles Capps, who has a daily syndicated radio broadcast, "Concepts of Faith," has written many best-selling books preaching the Prosperity Gospel. One of his books, *God's Creative Power for Finances,* gets right to the point. It's ironic that Christ taught:

> And again I say unto you, It is easier for a camel to go through the eye of a needle than for a rich man to enter into the kingdom of God. (Matthew 19:24)

So, where is the scriptural foundation that some say is proof that God wants us to prosper financially? One commonly quoted passage comes from John: "I am come that they might have life, and they might have it more abundantly" (John 10:10).

Did Jesus mean financial abundance? I don't think so. The

apostles were as poor as church mice. Jesus didn't even own a donkey! He had to borrow one for his triumphant ride into Jerusalem. He was even buried in a borrowed tomb. The abundance that Christ talks of is not material abundance. I believe he was talking about spiritual abundance. Christ spoke eloquently about those things we treasure: "For where your treasure is, there will your heart be also (Luke 12:34).

In reading or listening to the preaching of the Word, a healthy skepticism is in order. A preacher or writer may be extremely knowledgeable and sincere in their desire to spread God's word. But, there is only one who speaks "the whole truth, and nothing but the truth," and that is Jesus Christ. He *is* the Truth. We all need to pray for the gift of discernment. King Solomon prayed for wisdom, asking God, "Give therefore thy servant an understanding heart to judge thy people, that I may discern between good and bad" (1 Kings 3:9). And God answered him, saying, "Because thou hast asked this thing, and hast not asked for thyself long life; neither hast asked riches for thyself, nor hast asked the life of thine enemies; but hast asked for thyself understanding to discern judgment; behold I have done according to thy words" (1 Kings 3:11).

The cross is central to the Christian faith. It is much more than a symbol of death. It is a symbol of great love:

For God so loved the world, that he gave his only begotten Son, that whosoever believeth in him should not perish, but have everlasting life. (John 3:16)

The Incredible Shrinking Man

*S*omewhere along the line, "small" got a bad reputation. *These days, everything is big. You can buy a Big Mac and Super-size it to get a large fries and a large Coke. More and more Christians are choosing megachurches and listening to mass choirs. Every year, small cars get bigger. But it wasn't always that way. The scale of things was much smaller back in Christ's day. Jesus promised: "For where two or three are gathered together in my name, there am I in the midst of them" (Matthew 18:20).*

In emphasizing the power of faith, Christ said, "It is like a grain of mustard seed, which when it is sown in the earth, is less than all the seeds that be in the earth" (Mark 4:31).

Even God, when he spoke to Elijah, did so in "a still small voice" (1 Kings19:12).

In these days of American Idol, it is good to remember the value of humility. John the Baptist realized this. In testifying of Jesus, he said, "He must increase, but I must decrease" (John 3:30).

It is in their humility that a Christian is marked as a child of God.

She goes to your church. You might not know her name, but you know who I'm talking about. She's the one in the kitchen, preparing the refreshments for the coffee hour. Or maybe she sits quietly at a table in a back room, folding and stapling the church bulletins each week. She's the one who goes to visit the sick, without any fanfare. It doesn't make any difference whether she knows them or not. She remembers Christ's words: "I was sick and ye visited me" (Matthew 25:36). She's not looking for glory and is uncomfortable if you praise her.

Just how do we go about decreasing our self? Not by false

humility. False humility stinks to high heaven. Those exemplary Christians who quietly go about their business rarely talk about themselves. It's not necessarily that they are always quiet. They're just always busy doing. As we grow in God's grace, our thoughts stay on Jesus. It is not so much that we diminish ourselves by minimizing our value. It is in glorifying Christ that he is increased. The first sentence in Rick Warren's wonderful book, *A Purpose-driven Life,* says it all: "It's not about you." A sure sign of spiritual maturity is when a Christian is looking outward more than inward. If we are to increase Christ, we must be released from our self-centeredness.

In Paul's letter to the Colossians, he spoke directly about the virtues that identify a Christian. "Put on therefore, as the elect of God, holy and beloved, bowels of mercies, kindness, humbleness of mind" (Colossians 3:12). "And whatsoever ye do in word or deed, do all in the name of the Lord Jesus, giving thanks to God and the Father by him" (Colossians 4:17). Lest we seek glory for ourselves, it is best to remember that the only praise that matters is if, at the end of our lives, God says to us, "Well done, thou good and faithful servant" (Matthew 25:21).

Try Easier

*T*he message on the billboard caught my eye: "Nothing Is as Uncommon as Common Sense." Driving at sixty-five miles per hour, I didn't notice if the statement was attributed to anyone, but I recognized the truth in the saying. So, just what is common sense? Merriam-Webster defines it as: "Sound and prudent judgment based on a simple perception of the situation or facts." Albert Einstein had a more jaded view: "Common sense is the collection of prejudices acquired by age eighteen."

Back when I was taking a psychology course in college, I read of an experiment conducted with a group of student volunteers. There've been countless experiments with mice in mazes, trying to better understand problem solving. This time they used students. Instead of using a maze, they constructed a large round room with many doors. A student was led into the center of the room, and then the door through which they came in was locked. Only one door in the room was unlocked. Then, an electrical current was passed through the floor, creating a mild but uncomfortable shock. The student had to discover which door was unlocked in order to escape the room. The first reaction to the shock was the subject running to the nearest door and trying to open it. When they found that it was locked, they'd race to another door. Sometimes, after trying a door only to find it locked, the student would race to the center of the room, then turn around and try the same door again. I think the mice probably did better. Sometimes we try too hard.

When circumstances beyond our control destroy all our efforts to resolve a problem, we turn to the old sayings for encouragement. "If at first you don't succeed, try, try again." "Winners never quit and quitters never win." The Bible is rife with passages that seem to insure success. Christ encouraged us by saying:

> If ye have faith as a grain of mustard seed, ye shall say unto this mountain, Remove hence to yonder place; and it shall remove and nothing shall be impossible to you. (Matthew 17:20)

So, why do we so fail so often, even when we believe that we are trying to do God's will and have prayed for his help? Is it our lack of faith? Are Christ's promises empty words? After all, didn't he say, "Ask and ye shall receive, that your joy may be full"? (John 17:24).

We've all experienced times in our lives when we've almost killed ourselves trying to do something, and yet we failed. Each time that we were unsuccessful, we picked ourselves up, dusted ourselves off, and started all over again.

In my life there have been too many times when my dogged determination ended in frustration and failure. Trying again and again didn't work. In baseball, there's an old cliché that says, "The best trades are the ones you didn't make." That's true in our lives, too. Sometimes the best thing that happens to us is that we fail. God is surely watching over us, protecting us from succeeding in messing up our lives. God sees things differently than we do. We only see the moment. He sees our whole life spread before him. As God reminds us:

> For my thoughts are not your thoughts, neither are your ways my ways, saith the Lord. (Isaiah 57:8)

There are many reasons "success" eludes us, no matter how many times we try. One of the main reasons we fail is that we are not doing God's will. We are all capable of deluding ourselves into believing that what we want is really what God wants. What we are trying to do may even be good. That doesn't mean it's God's will. If you have been striving to do something that is not his will, it is only through God's mercy that you don't succeed.

Another common reason we don't succeed is that we have not waited on the Lord. If we are to do God's will, we have to wait on him: "Wait on the Lord, and keep his way" (Psalm 37:34).

Sometimes we fail because we are trying to do something that is not our job. God will not place us in a battle we cannot win. The words that Jehaziel spoke to the inhabitants of Judah and Jerusalem ring true for each of us to this day:

Thus saith the Lord unto you, Be not afraid nor dismayed . . . for the battle is not yours, but God's. (2 Chronicles 20:15)

Moses, when speaking to the Israelites, tried to calm their hearts by saying: "Fear ye not, stand still, and see the salvation of the Lord" (Exodus 14:13 KJV).

God does not expect us to do miracles. That's his business.

Perhaps the old saying about success needs some revisions for Christians: If at first you don't succeed, give it another try, and if that doesn't work, check with the Lord. You might ask him? "Is this really your will, God? If not, tell me, so I can stop beating my head against the wall." "If it is your will, let me know when you want me to try again." The Lord may need to prepare you more fully before you attempt to do it again. Don't get discouraged if you fail. Maybe you just need to try easier.

Kingdom Seekers

*H*ollywood has had a long love affair with kingdoms. In the movie Lost Horizon, *based on the popular novel by James Hilton, a plane crashes high in the snow-topped mountains of the Himalayas where the small band of travelers discover the beautiful Shangri-La. Shangri-La is the ultimate lost kingdom, where there is no knowledge of greed, war, or crime. Walt Disney built his own Magical Kingdom, fulfilling the fantasies of every child. The Indiana Jones' movies have captured the excitement of discovering lost kingdoms—most recently,* The Kingdom of the Crystal Skulls.

Christ calls us to seek a different kind of kingdom, one where the riches are of the heart.

Every time Reverend Perry would pose the question in Bible study class, "Where is the kingdom of God?" everyone seemed to freeze. Or maybe it was just me. No matter how many times he asked that question over the course of a year, there was always an awkward hesitation before someone answered. Sometimes, it took two or three tries before someone said, "The Kingdom of God is within you" (Luke 17:21). And I would mutter to myself, under my breath, "I've got to remember that!"

When Christ was questioned about his kingdom by Pontius Pilate, he answered, "My kingdom is not of this world." (John 18:36). Christ spoke about the kingdom of heaven more than one hundred times, so it was clearly important to him. Just how important was evidenced when he said:

Therefore take no thought, saying, What shall we eat? or, What shall we drink? or, wherewithal shall we be clothed? (For after all these things do the Gentiles seek) for your heavenly Father knoweth that ye have need of all these things. But seek ye first the kingdom of God, and his righteousness; and all these things shall be added unto you. (Matthew 6:31–33)

We are to seek after the kingdom of God and his righteousness *first*. So, where do we start looking? We must turn to Christ for guidance if we are to find his kingdom. As Christ often did, he taught about the kingdom of heaven in parables. In Matthew, he described the kingdom of heaven as "Like unto a great treasure hid in a field, the which when a man hath found it, he hideth it, and for joy thereof goeth and selleth all that he hath, and buyeth that field" (Matthew 13:44).

The kingdom of God is more precious than anything we possess. But, how do we go about seeking it? Maybe the Sermon on the Mount can give us some guidance. Who are those who shall gain the kingdom of heaven? "The poor in Spirit" (Matthew 5:3).

Christ doesn't mean that those who are "poor in Spirit" are not Spirit-filled. He means that they are humbled in the Spirit, recognizing that everything that they have is from God.

I thank you Father for the things you've done
All that I have belongs to you[29]

Those who are poor in Spirit recognize their dependence upon God. Theirs is an attitude of humility and thanksgiving. The kingdom of God is for "They which are persecuted for righteousness' sake" (Matthew 5:10).

Following Jesus isn't always going to be easy. But those who walk in righteousness can take comfort in knowing they will receive their reward, no matter how harshly they are persecuted. There is a special place in the kingdom of God for those who do his will:

Whosoever shall do and teach them (the commandments), the same shall be called great in the kingdom of heaven. (Matthew 5:19)

---

[29] "May I Abide in You" by Jerry Rasmussen

Notice the order Christ gives to doing and teaching; do first, and then teach. And the picture becomes clearer.

Finally, Christ says, "Whosoever shall not receive the kingdom of God as a little child shall in no wise enter therein" (Luke 18:17). Those who seek the kingdom of heaven must enter like a child. We are to be child*like*, not child*ish*.

> When I was a child, I spake as a child, I understood as a child, I thought as a child: but when I became a man, I put away childish things. (1 Corinthians 13:11)

In Matthew, Christ gives one of the qualities of a child that we must have in order to enter the kingdom of heaven: "Whosoever therefore shall humble himself as this little child, the same is greatest in the kingdom of heaven" (Matthew 18:4).

Like a child, we are to "Love God with all thy heart, and with all thy soul, and with all thy strength and with all thy mind" (Luke 10:27). Like a child, we are to have the utmost respect and reverence for God, never deeming ourselves worthy of standing in his presence.

For those who seek the kingdom of God with sincerity and commitment, all else will follow. That is important for us to remember. It is easy to get caught up in our desire to serve God, confusing busyness with holiness. We must trust God completely, so that we will not be overwhelmed with concern for our needs.

Why do you worry, when God has promised
That all who ask, they shall receive
There is no burden that is too heavy
If we will only trust and believe[30]

In trying to do all of these things, we seek to fulfill the prayer that our Lord taught to us, praying that "Thy kingdom come, thy will be done, In earth as it is in heaven" (Matthew 6:10).

---

[30] "The Way of the Lord" by Jerry Rasmussen

Most importantly, if we are to first seek the kingdom of God, we need to turn to our heavenly Father. As the songs says:

We are our heavenly Father's children
And we all know that he loves us one and all
If we are willing, he will teach us
His voice only, to obey no matter where[31]

Finally, if we wish to seek the kingdom of God, we should turn to his Word. As the song says, we can use the Bible to help us find our way:

I'm using my Bible for a road map[32]

The next time Reverend Perry asks, "Where is the kingdom of God?" I know what to say: It's in the Book; you can look it up.[33]

---

[31] "He Knows How Much We Can Bear" by Phyllis Hall
[32] "I'm Using my Bible as a Road Map" by Don Reno and Charles Schroeder
[33] Casey Stengel

A Lifetime Guarantee

*F*orever is a long time. There is nothing of this Earth that we can count on. Reverend Dennis Albrecht liked to tell a story of one of the first Bible study classes he taught as a young minister. He began the first class by inviting each member to talk about the passage in the Bible that gave them the greatest comfort in times of distress. As each member spoke, many referred to Psalm 23: "The Lord is my shepherd, I shall not want . . ." When it came his turn to speak, an elderly man said that the passage that always gave him strength was, "And it came to pass." He took that as a promise, not as a literary device to denote the passage of time.

All things of this Earth will *come to pass. In our insecurity, we seek for some comfort, a guarantee we can count on. For this, we can turn to Jesus. He promised: "I am with you always, even unto the end of the world" (Matthew 28:20).*

It never fails. Every time I buy something, the salesman tries to sell me an extended warranty. It seems like nothing is guaranteed for more than one year: more commonly, for no more than ninety days. Even if you buy an extended warranty, the longest guarantee that you can usually get is three years. I can still remember when I used to buy something, expecting it to last longer than that. That was before they came up with the idea of an extended warranty. Some warranties are for as long as you own the product. But, the "lifetime" warranty is the product's lifetime, not yours.

As you get older, lifetime guarantees take on a different meaning. You start wondering how long your own lifetime is guaranteed. If you're in your eighties, a lifetime guarantee doesn't mean as much as it did when you were in your twenties. I used to listen with amusement to my parents when they'd say, "This is the last car we'll buy." They ended up buying four "last cars." No one knows the number of their days. "This may be the last time, I don't know," as the Rolling Stones sang. When you're in your twenties, or even in your fifties, life seems to extend forward to an endless horizon. You think about career paths and find comfort in long-range planning. Dying is something you'll get around to someday, but right now, you're too busy.

Nowhere is the change in perspective more noticeable than in a nursing home. For many years, I've sung in health care facilities and senior residences, trying to bring at least a brief respite from the boredom and anxiety I see on so many faces. They're not singing, "The future's so bright, I gotta wear shades."[34] The future is intimidating. I remember one of the residents saying dryly, "The only way out of here is in a pine box."

Reverend Albrecht liked to say, "People start coming back to church when they get old, because they're cramming for finals." He always got a laugh out of that because people recognized the truth in the statement. When your lifetime guarantee looks like it may be running out, you're faced with a hard reality. Some people become bitter or depressed. They find the future threatening, and they feel there is nothing left to look forward to. And so, they look back. Those who are blessed seek their joy in what still remains. As my friend Art Thieme says, they accept a life of "diminished expectations." As I get older and start checking out my own warranty, I think of the way my parents lived the last years of their lives. Even though their daily activities were increasingly limited by failing health and strength, they were wise enough to realize that no matter how weak they were, they could still serve the Lord.

"They also serve who only stand and wait."[35]

You can still serve, even if you can only sit, or are confined to a bed.

Growing old can give a new perspective about the importance of listening to someone, holding their hand, or laughing at their jokes no matter how many times you've heard them. My wife and I have visited people in intensive care who still managed to offer

---

[34] From the song of that title, by Pat McDonald
[35] John Milton—Sonnet 19, "On His Blindness" 1652

encouragement and wisdom to the young nurses who came to them seeking their wisdom. Sometimes the patient does the healing.

The problem with a Lifetime Guarantee is that it expires when you do. And none of us knows our expiration date. God's Lifetime Guarantee doesn't have an expiration date because he promises eternity to those who give their lives to him.

You ask how I know this and how can it be?
When Christ he died up on Calvary
He said he'd be with us to the end of our days
He is the life, the truth and the way [36]

The Bible is filled with promises of eternal life. One of the most beloved statements of Christ's is found in John:

For God so loved the world that he gave his only begotten Son, that whosoever believeth in him should not perish, but have everlasting life. (John 3:16)

The comfort of Christ's promise is that death is a new beginning, not an end. If we can rejoice for a newborn child when they are brought into an imperfect and sometimes cruel world, how much more can we rejoice at the rebirth of a loved one who is entering paradise? The imagery of Revelation guides us in our understanding of what is to come for all of us:

Therefore are they before the throne of God, and serve him day and night in his temple: and he that sitteth on the throne shall dwell among them. They shall hunger no more, neither thirst any more; neither shall the sun light on them, nor any heat. For the Lamb which is in the midst of the throne shall feed them, and shall lead them unto living fountains of waters; and God shall wipe away all tears from their eyes. (Revelation 7:15–17)

An old song spoke wistfully about the "sweet mysteries of life." The mysteries of life here on earth can never compare to the sweetness of those of eternal life.

---

[36] "A True Story" by Jerry Rasmussen

Dry Behind the Ears

*B*ack in the Bible days, folks lived a long time. When someone says that a person is as old as Methuselah, they're talking old.

And Methuselah lived a hundred eighty and seven years and begat Lamech. And Methuselah lived after he begat Lamech seven hundred eighty and two years and begat sons and daughters. And all the days of Methuselah were nine hundred sixty and nine years; and he died. (Genesis 5:25–27)

Not that Methuselah was unusually old. Mehalaleel lived to be 895 years, and Noah was just a young stripling of 500 years when he begat Shem, Ham, and Japheth.

Skipping ahead to the time of Christ, Zechariah and Elisabeth were not young newlyweds when John the Baptist was conceived. As the Bible says,

And they had no child, because Elisabeth was barren, and they were both now stricken in years. (Luke 1:7)

I wrote about their miraculous conception in a song erroneously spelled Zacharias:

*Oh Zacharias was a fine old man, he had no daughter or son
Until the angel Gabriel to Zacharias did come*

CHORUS:
Zacharias, you better hold your tongue[37]

As they say, "age is just a number." In speaking of the righteous, David said of the aged:"They shall bring forth fruit in old age; they shall be fat and flourishing" (Psalm 92:14). "Fat and flourishing?" It's no wonder that Psalm 92 is rarely read from the pulpit.

Back when my Uncle Walt was still living, he was director of Cedar Crest, a retirement complex in my home town. He was a Methodist minister most of his life, and the position suited him well. His wife, Ruby, was the office manager, and after a lifetime of being a minister's wife, she could manage anything. When I was home visiting one summer, I went out with my mother and father to visit Uncle Walt and Aunt Ruby. They met us at the door, and led us to a small room at the end of the hall set aside for visitors. We no sooner sat down than a woman came rolling down the hall in a wheelchair at full tilt. When she made the turn and came through the doorway, she ran right over Uncle Walt's toes and he let out a small, dignified yelp. His years in the ministry had taught him to control his emotions.

Once the woman was in the room, she relaxed, her head slumped back, and she dozed off. A minute or so later, her eyes popped open and she was ready to visit. My aunt Ruby introduced us to the woman and said to her, "You just had a birthday; why don't you tell them how old you are?" The woman nodded and said proudly, "one hundred and five." And then she dozed off again for a minute or two. When her eyes popped open again, she continued her conversation without missing a beat. "You know, a man was here a couple of days ago, and I asked him, How old do you think I am?" He didn't want to guess my age (a wise man, indeed) so when I told him that I was one hundred and five, he said, "You don't look a day over one hundred." And she smiled broadly, brushing her hair back and smoothing a wrinkle in her cotton robe.

It's funny. Most women are flattered if you guess their age, if you say that you think they're younger than they are. Most of the men I know take pride in how old they are. They take each year added on

---

[37] "Zacharias"

to their age as an accomplishment. My friends Joe and Frankie in the Gospel Messengers love to tell everyone how old they are. Joe is eighty-four and Frankie eighty-two. I tell everyone that I'm the young kid in the group at seventy-three. And Joe and Frankie stand there beaming, just like that little one-hundred-and-five-year-young woman in the wheelchair. If someone had told Methuselah he didn't look a day over nine hundred, he would have felt hurt.

Not all people are "stricken" in years when they reach old age. They don't have the time for that kind of nonsense. They're too busy enjoying life. My mother was one of those people.

When I was kid growing up in the '40s, there was always music. It's not that we were a particularly musical family. My oldest sister, Marilyn, played violin for awhile and my sister Helen tried her hands at the old upright piano my parents bought. I played a below-average sweet potato, and was only slightly better on ukulele. But, our old Philco upright filled the air with all the popular hits of the war years. I'd cough up ten cents of my modest allowance to buy the latest issue of *The Hit Parade* magazine and knew all the songs by heart.

> *And the three mile crick was four miles long*
> *Back when I was young*
> *And I knew the words to every song*
> *Known to the human tongue*[38]

My mother loved to sing the old hymns, but my dad was never much for music.

As we kids grew up and moved out of the house one by one, the music died. For Mom, it wasn't the day that the Big Bopper and Richie Valens died in the plane crash. It was when Dad breathed a sigh of relief and said, "Finally, we can have some quiet around here." Mom's listening to music days were fading fast, and when they moved into an apartment and Dad was home all the time, they were pretty much over.

When my father died, back in 1997, I went home for his funeral. After the funeral service was over, Mom asked if I'd take her out to eat at Perkin's restaurant. It was one of her favorite restaurants but

---

[38] "Back When I Was Young," by Jerry Rasmussen

Dad refused to go there. Mixed in with the mourning was the unfamiliar scent of freedom, and Mom wanted to enjoy it. When we went to Perkin's, I ordered a burrito. Mom had never had one and her stomach was not the adventurous type, but she wanted to kick up her heels a little, so she ordered one, too. After dinner, we went over to Target and I bought Mom a stereo. She'd never had a CD player, so I bought her a sampling of music that I thought she'd like. I picked up a Lawrence Welk CD, one by Perry Como, and a CD of Strauss waltzes, which she'd always loved. When we got back to her apartment, I set everything up and showed her how to operate the CD player.

When I came down to the apartment the next morning, there was Mom leaning forward and listening intently to the radio. She had on a station that was playing rap and hip-hop music. She looked up as I came in the room and said, "I'm awfully out of date! The last time I listened to the radio they were playing Glen Miller."

Mom finally went home to Jesus when she was ninety-nine. That may not seem like much in comparison to Mister Methuselah, but she still had a good run. The last few years of her life she spent her days putting new wine into new bottles. And she brought forth much fruit.

Restless Hearts

*I*t seems like every time I turn around, they've identified another *medical problem. Over the years, when I'd talk to my mother, she'd often say that she had a bad night's sleep because her legs were bothering her. As we get older, muscles that were young and vital become rigid and inflexible. If we aren't on our guard, so do our attitudes about life. Now, modern science has identified the problem: we have Restless Leg Syndrome. And of course, there's a medication for it. The whole pharmaceutical industry seems driven by the desire to identify a never-ending list of new health problems, all of which can be resolved by taking yet another pill.*

All of us suffer from Restless Heart Syndrome. You know the symptoms. Something doesn't seem right in your life, but you just can't put your finger on it. It can keep you awake at night just as surely as restless legs. There is no pill that can cure Restless Heart Syndrome. But, there is a doctor you can turn to. The emptiness in your heart is not a medical problem. It is a lack of connection with the Lord. Turn to Jesus; in him you will find rest.

Just as the phrase, "the eyes of faith," moved me deeply when I first heard it; I was equally touched by a saying from another sermon of Rev. Albrecht. It was a few weeks before Christmas and in his sermon, Dennis used the phrase, "The heart is restless until it rests in Thee." That's a paraphrase of a line from *The Confessions of Saint Augustine*. Saint Augustine was a prodigal son, living a life of sin and immorality until he accepted Jesus Christ as his Savior. He knew all about a restless heart. We all do. It's that gnawing hunger that can only be satisfied by one thing: Jesus Christ. Until you accept Christ into your heart it will indeed be restless. But Jesus is patient. He'll wait until you've tried everything else, knowing that sooner or later you will realize where true peace lies.

Those two phrases became linked in my mind, and it was only a matter of time before God created a song in my heart, combining them:

And in the darkness, give me the eyes of faith
In my sorrow, send down your healing grace
And on my journey, may my path be straight
May my heart find rest in thee[39]

When we have exhausted the pleasures of this world, we turn to God to ease our hearts. Jesus tells us: "Lay not up for yourself treasures upon earth, where moth and rust doth corrupt, and where thieves break through and steal. But lay up for yourselves treasures in heaven, where neither moth nor rust doth corrupt, and where thieves do not break through nor steal. For where your treasure is, there will you heart be also." (Matthew 6:19–21)

In our restlessness, we pray that we may find peace: "But in every thing by prayer and supplication with thanksgiving, let your requests be made known to God. And the peace of God, which passeth all human understanding, shall keep your hearts and minds through Jesus Christ" (Philippians 4:6–7).

There is one cure for the restless heart. His name is Jesus. Christ, in speaking to his disciples, knowing that he was soon to be crucified, said, "These things I have spoken unto you, that in me ye might have peace" (John 16:13).

That wonderful peace is still there, for all who open their hearts to Christ.

---

[39] "May my Heart find Rest in Thee"

Sing Unto the Lord an Old Song

"*Sing unto the Lord a new song*"(Isaiah 42:10).
Deep in our hearts there is a desire to lift our voices in praise to the Lord. We seek new ways to express a love that is as old as the beginning of time. Music has always been at the heart of worship. The Book of Psalms is a collection of songs, hymns, poetry, and prayers. Even venerable old Moses was known to break into song on occasion, praising the Lord. "Then sang Moses and the children of Israel this song unto the Lord" (Exodus 15:1).

Just because we are encouraged to sing a new song doesn't mean that the Lord no longer likes to hear the old ones. For many people, it is the old songs that bind us together.

> *I like to sing those gospel songs my family used to sing*
> *In solid four-part harmony, we'd make the rafters ring*
> *We didn't need a hymnal 'cause we knew the songs by heart*
> *They formed a bond between us and we swore we'd never part*
>
> *There was a comfort in those words that still is there today*
> *A wisdom in the words we sang, to guide us on our way*
> *And friendships formed in harmony will last forever more*
> *Until we're reunited upon that golden shore*[40]

Old age can be a cruel mistress. It can rob us of our memories and separate us from those who love us most. Sometimes an old song can rekindle memories long since forgotten, taking us back to a happier time in our lives. I think of the elderly woman in a nursing home whowas paralyzed and strapped in her wheel chair. She was

---

[40] "I Like to Sing those Gospel Songs" by Jerry Rasmussen

locked in her body and couldn't move, but her mind was free to travel to a time still remembered.

> *And sometimes the memories come back with a song*
> *Just as surely as if she were there*[41]

All that it took was an old song.

My wife, Ruth, and I went to visit our friend Joe's wife, Corrie, after church today. Corrie has Alzheimer's Disease. It had been quite awhile since our last visit and she'd lost a lot of ground. Most days when Joe goes to visit her (and he's never missed a day), she doesn't open her eyes and rarely utters a comprehensible sentence. More often than not she doesn't recognize visitors.

When we arrived at the nursing home, they were just bringing Corrie down the corridor. She was slouched back in her wheelchair, seemingly oblivious to everything. Old Mister Alzheimer had stolen her away, leaving us with a pale imitation of the quick-witted and fun-loving woman we had known and loved for so many years. We brought a plant and a card for her, and Joe tried to make her aware that we were there. She had her eyes open and was wearing her glasses, but it was difficult to know what images were registering in her mind. Despite all of Joe's loving efforts to talk with her, she didn't respond, other than to occasionally utter a low cry as if she were in pain. Joe kept asking her if she had any pain, but the questions hung there in the warm corridor air, fading away with no answer. Joe asked me to read the card to Corrie, so I squatted down in front of her wheelchair and read it to her, telling her how much we love her and that we are keeping her in prayer. With that, she attempted to string together a few words into a sentence, and for the first time, I felt that I was breaking through to her. Whatever remained of Corrie was trying to reach out to me. After talking to her for a couple of minutes, I squatted down next to her again, resting one hand on hers that was laying limply on the arm of her wheelchair and placing my other hand gently on her shoulder. I leaned forward and looked deep into her eyes and began to sing.

---

[41] "Tortoiseshell Comb" by Jerry Rasmussen

Safe Keeping

We've all known the terror of a nightmare where we are threatened by some evil thing and cannot run or use our limbs to protect ourselves. We are completely helpless. It is even more terrifying when we have no idea why we are being attacked, or by whom. One restless night, I came face to face with a power I could not understand or protect myself from.

I was standing there, staring out the window into the darkness, when a face suddenly materialized before me. The house was silent, and yet I heard no sound of the man who had mysteriously appeared. He turned away from the window and I could see him walking around the house toward the front door. Anxiety rose up in my throat. Where was I? The room was unfamiliar and I had no idea why I was there. I heard the front door open and waited with dread until the man came walking through the doorway into the room. He wasn't physically imposing and he had a slight smile on his face, but there was something threatening about him. "Where is it?" he asked. "Where is what?" I answered. Once again he asked, "Where is it?" "I have no idea what you're talking about," I said. "There's no sense in pretending like you don't know; I want it." I still had no idea what "it" was, but even if I did, I decided that I wouldn't want to give it to him.

As he started moving toward me, the smile turned more menacing. I noticed a baseball bat leaning in the corner and reached over to grab it. "There's no sense resisting," he said. "Give it to me." "I'll give it to you, all right, but it may not be what you want," I said, raising the baseball bat over my shoulder. As he stepped forward, I took a swing for the seats and hit him squarely on the side of his head. The force of the impact sent shockwaves up my arms and across my back, yet he stood there completely unaffected, with that same sweet, sick smile on his face. He took a few more shorts steps toward me with his hand outstretched, and I let him have it again, this time with all the strength that I could muster. Despite the force of the blow, he showed no sign of discomfort. I was the one who was hurting now. One more step and another swing, and I realized that I had no way of stopping him. And then he stopped, and as suddenly as he had appeared, he turned and left the room. I could hear him as he closed the front door, and for a moment the house was plunged back into silent darkness. Only the faint light through the picture window illuminated the room.

As I stood there trying to understand what had happened, I heard the front door opening once more, and my heart was filled with dread. As a woman came around the corner and entered the room, I leaned the baseball bat back against the corner cabinet. I couldn't imagine hitting a woman with a bat, no matter how evil she might be. I could see that I was on my own. She was a tall woman, dressed in what used to be called toreador pants and a short jacket. She was thin and angular and her body moved in sections, as if she wasn't used to inhabiting it. Rather than threatening me, she spoke in a sweet, reasonable, comforting tone. "I'm sorry about how that man acted," she said with a slight smile. "There was no need to threaten you. I'm sure that I can offer you a generous compensation if you will sell it to me." I still had no idea what "it" was, but I was no more inclined to sell "it" than I was to let someone take it away from me. She said, "I'll give you much more than it is actually worth." When I told her that I had no intention of parting with it, her voice took on a hard, cruel tone. "You'd be wise to take my offer, because if you don't accept it, I will just have to take it away from you."

By then I was getting angry. I realized from my experience with the first man that there was no way that I could fight the woman. I had no idea what she and the man were, but they were certainly not of this Earth. "Before I'd give it to you, I'd destroy it," I answered, and I could see she was getting very angry. "Or maybe I'll just give it to someone else who you don't know, and it will be someone that I know would never give it to you, even if you found them." "Oh, I'd have no trouble finding them," she answered. "No one is strong enough to resist me." "Well, I am!" I spoke, my voice rising as I stared directly into her eyes. She shrugged her shoulders and said, "I'll give you time to think it over, but I'll be back to collect it." As she angled her way across the room, my strength drained from me. I had spoken out of anger and fear, but I knew, deep in my heart, that no one could resist her for long. Certainly not me.

I stood there alone in the darkened room, my mind racing. Who could I give it to who would protect it, who was invulnerable to temptation or threats of violence? Not a soul came to mind. And then the warning bell of my cell phone went off, notifying me that the battery was low, and I woke up.

For a moment I lay there completely disoriented until the old familiar outlines of the bedroom furniture came into focus. I was filled with an indescribable dread and not a little thanksgiving that my cell phone had rescued me from such a disturbing nightmare. I got up, went over and took my cell phone out of my pants pocket, and carried it downstairs to recharge the battery. My soul-battery was the one that really needed recharging. After plugging the adapter into the cell phone and setting it up to be recharged, I sank back into my recliner and asked myself, "What was that all about?" I was still shaken, and asked the Lord to reveal to me what the "it" was that was so precious. And who the wraiths (or whatever they were) were. And then it became obvious. The "it" was my soul. The devil had come to tempt me to give him/her my soul.

First he sent one of his minions to try to scare it out of me. The first word that came to mind was that he was a demon. But demons are Greek in origin. This guy looked more like he came from New Jersey. He must have been like one of the devils that Christ was always casting out of people. And the woman in sections? She was the Devil him/herself. If he can appear as a snake, I guess he can appear as a woman if he wants to.

As I sat in the chair, lost in prayer, I tried to figure out the meaning of the dream. I generally don't put much stock in dreams. I'm more likely to dismiss them as an aftereffect of too much pepperoni pizza. But this was different. It was too disturbing to reject out of hand. We are all helpless when we come face-to-face with the Devil. Don't think he's going to come dressed in red long underwear, wearing a black goatee and nothing else. He discarded those costumes long ago. He can appear in any form he wants, and he is very insidious. We are no match for his power. But Jesus is. Jesus went mano a mano with the Devil in the wilderness, and no amount of temptation or threats could weaken Christ's resolve.

"And Jesus answered and said unto him, 'Get thee behind me, Satan; for it is written, Thou shalt worship the Lord the God, and him only shalt thou serve' " (Luke 4:8). I was in need of a little ministering to, myself.

As often happens, the words to one of my favorite old hymns came to mind:

> *Jesus, lover of my soul*
> *Let me to thy bosom fly*
> *While the nearer waters flow*
> *While the tempest still is high*[43]

We are not helpless. Whom can we give our soul to who will keep it safe, who is invulnerable to threats of violence? Only Jesus. Nobody does you like Jesus.

---

[43] "Jesus, Lover of my Soul" by Simeon B. Marsh

Everyday Miracles

*T*hey called it the Miracle of Coogan's Bluff. It was the last half of the ninth inning of a "sudden death" playoff game to determine who would win the National League Championship when Bobby Thomson of the New York Giants strode to the plate. Ralph Branca was on the mound for the Brooklyn Dodgers. He peered in to get his sign, reared back, and fired the ball toward home plate. With a mighty swing of his bat, Thomson drove the ball over the fence, and the crowd went wild. Russ Hodges, the Giant's announcer, made the call that would be remembered forever: The Giants win the pennant!, the Giants win the Pennant!, the Giants win the pennant!, the Giants win the pennant! It was called "The shot heard 'round the world." And Bobby Thomson earned a permanent place in baseball lore.

Many years ago, the Israelites found themselves in a different type of "sudden death" situation. Fleeing from Pharaoh's army, they found their escape blocked by the Red Sea. As often happens in such a dire situation, the Israelites looked for someone to blame.

"And they said unto Moses, 'Because there were no graves in Egypt, hast thou taken us away to die in the wilderness?' " (Exodus 14:11)

Even though they were facing imminent death, they couldn't resist being sarcastic. If ever anyone needed a miracle, it was Moses. Moses called out to God and God told him to command the sea to part: "And Moses stretched out his hand over the sea, and the Lord caused the sea to go back by a strong east wind all that night, and made the sea dry land, and the waters were divided" (Exodus 14:21).

Not all miracles are as dramatic as the parting of the Red Sea, or even Bobby Thomson's home run. When you get right down to it, *most things that are called "miracles" these days aren't miracles at all. Merriam-Webster defines a miracle as: "An extraordinary event manifesting divine intervention in human affairs." I don't think that God had anything to do with Thomson's home run, and I feel confident that he takes no credit for creating Miracle Whip salad dressing. That doesn't mean that God doesn't intervene in our daily lives. Miracles still happen.*

It was a long time coming. I had come through a brutal divorce that lasted two years. What little savings I'd had were long since exhausted and I was more deeply in debt than I had ever been in my life. I was driving an old Pinto station wagon, which was held together with bailing wire, two-by-fours, and prayers. It had been over two years since I'd had a salary increase at work and I had two sons to raise. But finally the day came. I received word at work that a retroactive salary increase had been approved, and I had a check for several thousand dollars clutched firmly in my hand. With joyful heart and prayers of thanksgiving to God, I put my sons in the car to drive down to the bank to deposit the check.

After we left the bank, I walked out to the car with a bounce in my step. The Lord had lifted a great burden from my shoulders. As I was backing out of the parking space, I noticed the car behind me, waiting impatiently for me to pull out. It was a small parking lot and spaces were hard to find. In my hurry, I stepped hard on the gas, and it sounded like the whole exhaust system erupted. My poor old Pinto was shaking like she had the fits, and the noise was deafening. I managed to finish backing up and drove out of the parking lot, my nerves on edge. There was only one thought in my mind; I had to try to get the car down to my mechanic before it completely gave up the ghost. Even though I was upset about the car, my heart was filled with thanksgiving. I knew that God was with me. As the Bible says: "All things work together for good to them that love God" (Romans 12:28).

God had been so good to me! He'd carried me through the darkest time of my life, and had given me the strength and resources to provide a meager, but hope-filled home for my sons. And just when my Pinto looked like she was ready to breathe her last breath, God had provided me with the money to buy a new used car. All these thoughts were rushing through my head as I tried to talk to my sons. The noise from the exhaust system was deafening, and I had to shout in order for my son Gideon to hear me, even though he was sitting in the front seat right next to me. As I started to shout, "See how good God is, He—" the exhaust system suddenly went back to its old, familiar, puttery self. I turned to Gideon and finished the sentence, "See how good God is; he provided us with the money so that we can buy another car, and now he's miraculously healed our Pinto." Gideon didn't believe a word of it. "Aw, Dad, we probably just hit a bump in the road that shook the muffler back into place!" "Oh ye of little faith!" I answered. Looking in the rearview mirror, I could see the street disappearing behind me, smooth as glass. They'd just repaved the road and there wasn't a bump to be seen. And that's the way God works. Not all miracles are as dramatic as parting the Red Sea, but the message is the same:

God is in charge.

Now, it could just as easily be argued that what I believed was a miraculous healing of my Pinto's exhaust system was no more of a miracle than Bobby Thomson's home run. That's the thing about miracles. You accept them on faith. They can't be proven, and they certainly can't be summoned, despite our most fervent prayers.

Reading the accounts of Christ when he performed miracles, at first it appears that they happened because of the believer's faith. Matthew recounts the story about the woman who had been diseased with an issue of blood for twelve years. She believed that if she could but touch the hem of Christ's garment, she would be healed.

But when Jesus turned him about, and when he saw her he said, Daughter, be of good comfort; thy faith hath made thee whole. (Matthew 9:22)

Christ also stated that:

If ye have faith as a grain of mustard seed, ye shall say unto this mountain, Remove hence to yonder place; and it shall remove. (Matthew 17:20)

The danger in seeking miracles based on the strength of our faith is that when a prayer seems to go unanswered and the miracle never happens, we may fault our faith as not being strong enough. After all, Christ used the phrase, "Oh, ye of little faith" as often as he did "Thy faith hath made thee whole." Miracles are God's call. It's all right that we pray for miracles. They happen every day. God wants to know our hearts, and he is touched by our love and compassion. But he said, "For my thoughts are not your thoughts, neither are your ways my ways" (Isaiah 55:8), and, "As for God, his way is perfect" (2 Samuel 22:31).

Not every mountain that we tell to "Remove hence to yonder place," is going to heed our command. Sometimes we have to pray,

Lord, don't move the mountain, but give me the strength to climb And Lord, don't take away my stumbling block, but lead me all around[44]

When God reaches out his hand and moves your mountain, all that you can do is praise him. Don't ask questions. And if he doesn't, know that God in his infinite love will give you the strength to climb it.

And by the way, miracles in the Old Testament apparently weren't as closely identified with faith. It's interesting to note that the word "faith" appears a grand total of two times in the Old Testament. It's found 244 times in the New Testament.

---

[44] "Lord Don't Move the Mountain" by Doris Akers and Mahalia Jackson

Dump Trucks, Hobos, and Jesus

I've *always found the topic of evangelism somewhat of a puzzlement. Yes, Christ calls us to evangelize. His Great Commission tells us to preach the gospel: "Go ye into all the world, and preach the gospel to every creature" (Mark 16:15).*

But, what does that mean, exactly? I know that we are to let our light shine. Christ spoke about that in the Sermon on the Mount:

> *Ye are the light of the world. A city that is set on a hill cannot he hid. Neither do men light a candle, and put it under a bushel, but on a candlestick; and it giveth light unto all that are in the house. (Matthew 5:15)*

When I look at all the things that are done in the guise of evangelism, I realize how dangerous the whole practice can be. I've heard TV evangelists say that Hurricane Katrina was an act of God as a punishment for a Gay Pride parade that was scheduled to be held in New Orleans. Is that what evangelism is all about? I surely hope not.

What is our responsibility in evangelizing? Many years ago in my confusion, I asked my pastor if he would devote one of our adult Bible study classes to the topic. When he broached the subject to our class and asked how we thought we should evangelize in our lives, a friend of mine was the first to speak. He said that he didn't like talking about religion with nonbelievers. He just tried to live a good life, believing that the way that he lived would draw people to God. Certainly, people measure our words by our actions, and we all pray that others might see Christ in us, but there must be more to evangelism than that. I commented that I had friends who lived exemplary lives who were atheists. I certainly wouldn't consider

115

converting to atheism because of the good that I saw in them.

Everyone has had the experience of trying to discuss religion with nonbelievers only to end up frustrated and hurt. Worse yet, it seemed that the nonbeliever was even further from Christ after the conversation. Not speaking about Jesus doesn't seem to be a viable response to that experience. Not speak about Jesus?

> *If I cannot speak for Jesus, I'd rather die . . . Oh, help me, Lord*
> *If I cannot speak for Jesus, I'd rather die . . . Oh, Lord*
> *If I can't stand with a folded arm*
> *Tell you how God bore his cross alone*
> *If I cannot speak for Jesus, I'd rather die*[45]

Part of the problem, I believe, is that we are not saviors. There is only one Savior. It is not within our power to "convert" anyone, either. That's the work of the Holy Spirit. After the Bible study class, I felt that I had more questions than I did before we went in. When I expressed my uncertainty to my pastor about how we are to evangelize, he gave me the wisest advice of all: Don't go looking for evangelism; evangelism will find you. And he was right. Evangelism finds us in the most unlikely places. It can be the sharing of just a few words. If they are put on our heart by the Holy Spirit, He can use us to help others come to Christ. "Therefore, be ye always ready." Matthew 24:44 is sound advice. You never know when God will place someone in your path who will be receptive to his word.

Evangelism is serious business. It takes constant prayer and study of the scripture. We are all called upon to evangelize, whether we are ordained ministers or just minister to people. We need to pray that the Lord puts the words in our mouth, that we may speak with his wisdom, not our own.

So, how do we evangelize? That depends upon how the Lord uses us. We all have different gifts. Some may evangelize by their actions, doing for "the least of" others what they would do for Christ. Some have the gift of speech and may be called to the ministry. For some, writing or music may be a talent to be used for evangelism. Others may be moved to reach out through phone calls, cards, or even e-

---

[45] "Speak for Jesus" as recorded by the Five Blind Boys of Mississippi

mails. Call it e-vangelism. Sometimes, just a hand resting gently on the shoulder of someone who is distressed can be an act of evangelism.

On this particular morning, a casual conversation I had with a total stranger naturally led to talking about Jesus.

He was standing there at the fence, with his hands on the upper rail, bracing his body with one foot up on the lower rail. He was engrossed in the activity before him and didn't notice me as I approached. There was a steady stream of large dump trucks hauling loads of fill up the slope of the hill, and a bulldozer grading the area. After almost a week of rain, everyone was out enjoying the first signs of spring. The magnolias and cherry trees were in full blossom and a pair of Baltimore orioles were busy building their nest in a small grove of trees near the walkway. A couple of boats were anchored in the river, and the men were leisurely casting their lines into the water. It didn't look like they were in any hurry to get a bite. The only sound I heard was the rumbling of the trucks disturbing an otherwise peaceful morning.

As I approached him, he turned to leave his watch, and I called out to him, "Good morning! They've got a mighty big job there."

He answered my greeting and said, "What are they trying to do, fill the whole area?"

"Naw, they're building up the slope so that they can widen Main Street to add a third lane," I said. And the conversation was rolling. He resumed his spot at the fence and I joined him. We stood there for awhile, talking about the plans for rebuilding downtown Derby. The man asked if I'd lived in Derby all of my life and I told him, "No, we moved up here six years ago."

"I grew up here," he said. "I remember when this whole area was still wild, and there was a hobo camp down on Sullivan's Island. My Mother used to warn me about going down there, but the guys were all friendly, and they were always happy to take the time to sit and tell me stories. They used to have gardens down there, and they sold their vegetables alongside the highway."

"I've noticed that it is often the people who have the least who are most willing to share," I said. "In the hobo camps, everyone had a colorful nickname. They called Jesus "Jerusalem Slim." I guess they figured that Jesus would feel right at home in a hobo camp, because he spent a lot of time on the road. I'm a musician, and I wrote a song about Jesus," I said, and I recited a few lines of the song to him.

You could find him by the campfires late at night
Or wading in the water in the morning light
He always took the time to lend a hand
He was kinda slow moving for a traveling man

No sooner did he come, and he'd be gone
And he never had a home to call his own
So if you get in trouble, you can call on him
'Cause you never had a friend like Jerusalem Slim[46]

And as we stood there in the early morning sunshine, I found myself talking about dump trucks and hobos and Jesus. Evangelism had found me.

---

[46] "Jerusalem Slim"

Give Me a Call When You Get Home

*T*here's something about the thought of going home that brings on a rush of emotions. As a kid, the one popular Christmas song that hit me the hardest was "I'll be Home for Christmas." It was hard for me to even imagine being away from home at Christmastime, and the song always put a lump in my throat. In many black churches, funerals are called "home-going" services. Even though we have no idea what heaven will be like, there is a hunger in our hearts to go there. There are times in our lives when we feel like we're going home, even if it's to a place we've never been to. Many years ago, I wrote a song about settlers moving west in prairie schooners. They were traveling into the unknown, and yet they felt that they were going home.

> Ships on the prairies that never sailed the seas
> Carrying all that they owned
> Sailing for mountains that they'd never seen
> Sailing away to home[47]

Jesus comforted us by saying, "In my Father's house are many mansions; if it were not so, I would have told you. I go to prepare a place for you (John 14:2).

If "home is where the heart is," then "I intend to make heaven my home."

"Give me a call when you get home. I just want to know that you got there all right." We've all said that to someone we love when they were traveling somewhere. It doesn't matter how far they're

---

[47] "Ships on the Prairies"

going. It might be a ten-minute drive on a snowy winter's night, or a trip overseas. It's a relief to hear from them when they get there. It puts our mind at ease.

Of all the journeys that we take in life, the longest one is our last journey home. My wife and I shared that journey with my mother through the summer and fall of 2006, along with the rest of our family. The old hymn says:

You've got to walk that lonesome valley
You've got to walk it by yourself
Ain't nobody here can walk it for you
You've got to walk that lonesome valley by yourself[48]

There is a lot of truth in that statement, but it isn't the whole truth. In Psalm 23, David wrote about that lonesome valley, offering comforting words of encouragement that God would be there by our side.

Yea, though I walk through the valley of the shadow of death, I will fear no evil: for thou art with me: thy rod and thy staff they comfort me. (Psalm 23:4)

Mom had the company of God on her long journey home. Sometime back in the '60s I wrote a song, "I'll Be Home." The lyrics to that song kept coming back to me in mom's final weeks, and they seemed to be her words as much as mine:

There's a dark road ahead that I wearily tread
And the night is cold
But his face I can see, and it beckons to me
And I believe all I've been told

Though temptation is great, I will not turn away
I must journey on
For the end is near, and death holds no fear
For I know what lies beyond

---

[48] "You've Got to Walk that Lonesome Valley"—traditional

Mom knew where she was going, and as she got closer to the end of the road, you could hear the excitement building in her voice. She began having visions of being reunited with her mother, who died when Mom was just thirteen years old, and Dad was there to greet her, too. Most of all, she was looking forward to sitting down to "have a little talk with Jesus."[49]

Despite the increasing desire to go home to Jesus, Mom wanted to hold on until she could celebrate her ninety-ninth birthday. We hadn't seen her in almost a year, and I think that she knew in her heart it would be our last chance to be together. She just wanted the chance to say good-bye.

The week we spent with Mom celebrating her ninety-ninth birthday was very sweet. She hadn't been out of Assisted Living where she had her room for almost a year. One of the first things she wanted us to do for her was to take her for a ride in the country. That was always a great love of Mom's and Dad's. They knew every tree, rock, creek, woods, and farm within a fifty-mile area. They'd go for rides in the summer to favorite places where Dad would collect wild plums, blackberries, wild asparagus, or mushrooms. In the fall, Dad knew where every hickory tree was within driving distance, and he'd collect bushel baskets full of nuts that he'd spend half the winter in the basement patiently cracking open. He'd end up with several quarts of hickory nuts to share with the family by the time spring rolled around. Just driving through the country was pleasure enough, in itself. We took Mom down along the River Road and through Afton, where her father and mother had a farm when she was young. Then we drove down narrow country roads, with Mom pointing out homes of old friends or places where Dad had gone fishing or hunting. Though we didn't speak about it, I think we all realized that the drive through the countryside might be the last one she'd take— and it was.

The night of September 12 was a dark one for Mom. Her breathing was becoming more labored and her heartbeat was slowing down dangerously. As she lay there in bed in her room with the end of the road finally in sight, the ceramic angel lamp on the windowsill next to her bed suddenly came on by itself. Mom had an angel to

---

[49] "Just a Little Talk with Jesus" by Cleavant Derricks

guide her in that final, dark night. And Jesus welcomed her home.

When Reverend John Froiland, chaplain at Cedar Crest where Mom lived, came into her room that morning, he noticed that a book I'd sent her was lying open. It was *My Utmost for His Highest* by Oswald Chambers. It was opened to a scriptural reading from Matthew: "Come unto me all ye that labour and are heavy laden, and I will give you rest" (Matthew 11:28).

And he knew that all was well with mom's soul. She'd gone home to Jesus.

All my sorrow and pain will not be in vain
When I reach my goal
When he takes my hand, then I'll understand
And his love will cleanse my soul[50]

And when Mom got home, she gave me a call, just to let me know that she was all right.

---

[50] "I'll Be Home" by Jerry Rasmussen

Knowing Jesus

*W*e are all in danger of being like those of whom Christ spoke who "hearing, they hear not, neither do they understand" (Matthew 13:13). We can sit in church every Sunday, our minds drifting off, only half-hearing the message, or even worse—hearing only what we want to hear.

Many years ago, a friend of mine gave me some advice, spoken with the greatest of conviction. She said, "You should love your husband or wife more than God."

I asked her, "What ever became of the first commandment? 'And thou shalt love the Lord thy God with all thy heart, and with all thy soul, and with all thy mind and with all thy strength' "? (Mark 12:30). I told her "You should love God more than anyone else," and she responded, "Aren't you getting carried away?"

"No," I answered. Christ was very clear about who we are to love most:

> *He that loveth father or mother more than me is not worthy of me; and he that loveth son or daughter more than me is not worthy of me. (Matthew 10:37)*

My friend had spent a lifetime going to church, but hadn't understood the greatest of all commandments.

> *Billows may roll, breakers may dash*
> *I shall not sway because he holds me fast*
> *So dark my days, clouds in the sky*
> *Still it's all right because he walks by my side*
> *Oh, do you know him?*[51]

---

[51] "Do You Know Him" by Mary Lou Parker

That's a good question. Do I really know Jesus? Knowing Jesus is more than knowing about Jesus. In this instance, "knowing" is more about having a relationship with Jesus than it is about knowledge of his life and teachings. I know agnostics and atheists who are more knowledgeable about Jesus than some Christians.

How do we come to know someone? Most importantly, by spending time with them. No matter how much we read about Jesus, we will never know him if we don't spend time with him in prayer and contemplation. Christ stands and waits at every door. It is simply a matter of inviting him to come in.

Behold, I stand at the door, and knock; if any man hear my voice, and open the door, I will come in to him, and will sup with him, and he with me. (Revelation 3:20)

In coming to know Jesus, we come to know his Father, too. The apostle John recounts a conversation where Christ is speaking to the Pharisees, "I am one that bear witness of myself, and the Father that sent me, ye should have known my Father also. Then said unto him, Where is thy Father? Jesus answered, Ye neither know me, nor my Father; if ye had known me, ye should have known my Father also" (John 8:18–19).

When Philip asked Christ, "Lord, show us the Father, and it sufficeth us," Christ responded, "He that hath seen me hath seen the Father" (John 14:8–9).

God is revealed to us in the scriptures through his son Jesus. Daily reading and reflection on the Word is at the heart of coming to know Jesus. We need to understand Christ's teachings if we are to know God. Christ chastised the Pharisees when they tried to trap him by questioning him about the resurrection, asking which of seven men that had been married to a seven-times widowed woman would be her husband in heaven.

He answered them, saying, "Do ye not therefore err, because ye know not the scriptures, neither the power of God?" (Mark 12:24).

We can come to know Jesus, not only through the scriptures but through the writings of others who can share their insights with us. Daily readings are a wonderful way to grow in the knowledge of Jesus. My wife and I treasure our morning reading and conversations together. We find *My Utmost for His Highest* by Oswald Chambers especially insightful, and it is one of our most beloved blessings for breakfast. There are many other writings that have helped us to come to know Jesus better.

For many Christians, hymns and gospel music speak to their hearts in a special way. Favorite lines like, "The battle is not yours, but mine, said the Lord," or "Stand still and see the salvation of the Lord" have helped to carry me through difficult times by reminding me of God's power.

Just as there is a time for quiet reflection, there is a time to celebrate our faith in the sweet communion of the saints with our friends and family. We are all members of one body, and we can help each other to come to know Christ in a way that we may never be able to find on our own. "So we being many, are as one body in Christ, and every one members of one another" (Romans 12:5).

Christ often spoke of himself as the good shepherd, and his followers as his flock. It is a wonderful image of Christ as our protector, willing to lay down his life for us. In gathering together, we give comfort to each other and help each other to grow in the knowledge of our Lord. "I know my sheep and am known of mine" (John 10:14).

Seek Christ through prayer, reading, music, and communion with other lovers of Christ, until he becomes as natural a part of your life as breathing in and out. It is the best thing that we do.

Love Lifts the Lover

*A*nd Jesus said,

 "Then shall the King say unto them on his right hand, Come, ye blessed of my Father, inherit the kingdom prepared for you from the foundation of the world: For I was ahungered, and ye gave me meat . . . .Then shall the righteous answer him, saying, Lord, when saw we thee ahungered and fed thee?

> *"And the King shall answer and say unto them, Verily I say unto you, Inasmuch as ye have done it unto the least of these my brethren, ye have done it unto me.Then shall he say unto them on the left hand, Depart from me ye cursed, into everlasting fire, prepared for the devil and his angels: For I was ahungered and ye gave me no meat." (Matthew 25:34–35,37,40–41)*

My wife, Ruth, and I spent today in New York City. Among other things we did, we went on a quest for a McDonald's. We'd seen a program on television listing the top ten McDonald's restaurants and one of them is in New York City. From what I remember, the McDonald's in Hell didn't make the list, but I hear their Big Macs are delicious. They're all flame-broiled and are served on small pitchforks, but I don't want to go there. When we were in Asheville, North Carolina, we went to the McDonald's across the street from the Biltmore Estate, where they have a fireplace and a player piano and the décor is reflective of the Estate. The one in New York City is supposed to have live entertainment and waitresses.

 Not knowing the address of the McDonald's we were looking for, we trekked from one McDonald's to the next, asking the people in each one if they knew where the fabled McDonald's was located.

We never did find it. By the time our search for the holy broil fell through, I was hungry. We were at the fourth or fifth McDonald's, and we were tired of walking, so I suggested we eat there.

No sooner had we sat down than a young black man approached us, asking for change. You could tell that he wasn't "seeding" the pot like they do in tip mugs, putting singles and five dollar bills in to keep you from throwing in a nickel. This young man had a dime, a nickel, and two pennies in his hand. I didn't see him approaching, so when he asked "Could you give me some change?" I shook my head, no. After he moved on, I felt the desire to give him something, but I didn't just want to give him some pocket change. When I pulled out my billfold and opened it, the first thing I saw was a five-dollar bill. And I thought, Why not? He needs it a lot more than I do. I took it out, walked over to the young man who by then had asked another dozen people with no success, and placed the five-dollar bill in his hand. He stuck it in his pocket without looking, and then embraced me, repeating "God Bless you, brother!" over and over again. I thanked him and told him that God does, and wished him a good day.

When he left, I sat down to finish my McChicken Sandwich, my McFries and my McCoffee. Not long afterward, the young man appeared again beaming from ear to ear. Apparently, he'd gone outside and fished the bill out of his pocket, expecting it to be a dollar bill only to discover that it was a five. He was so excited! He thanked Ruth and me repeatedly and once more asked God to bless us. It was a sweet experience.

When I lived in New York City, I found myself increasingly deadened to the people around me. It's hard to avoid becoming that way when you live there. It was the primary reason why I felt I had to get out of the city. Old voices would have said, "He's just going to use that money to buy drugs." And who knows, maybe he was. But somehow, I didn't think so.

Besides, thinking had nothing to do with it. It was an act of love.

Later, I remembered that Ruth and I had watched *Sullivan's Travels* the night before. The movie takes place during the depression and there is a scene where Sullivan walks through the slums, giving five-dollar bills to people who were down-and-out. We may not be that far away from a depression here, and maybe the image stayed in my mind. Whatever prompted me to pull out the five-dollar bill, I felt good about it. It reminded me of the chorus of a song I wrote a long time ago.

Love may be fickle, Love may be vain
Ignored or rejected, but all the same
Whatever the cost, love is never in vain
For love lifts the lover[52]

And I felt lifted.

It doesn't say in the Bible how the people on the left hand responded to Christ's teachings about the needy, but I imagine they said something like this:

"What are you talking about? The guy said he was hungry, but he looked like a drunk to me. He wouldn't have used the money to get something to eat, anyway. He would have bought a bottle of wine. I work hard for my money. Why should I give it to someone who's too lazy to work?"

When you feel that God is putting it on your heart to help someone, don't analyze it. Just do it.

---

[52] "Love Lifts the Lover"

The Cosmos and the Checkout Clerk

I *was talking with my old friend Reverend Dennis Albrecht the other day. It's been many years since we last talked, but it felt like only a few days had passed. Dennis moved away and we'd lost contact with each other. I tracked him down through my old church where he was my pastor. It was Dennis who first encouraged me to write, and I felt the need to rekindle our friendship and express my appreciation for all that he'd done for me.*

The old enthusiasm was still there. Dennis talked about his reading and writing about God's revelation in the universe. He mentioned a book he'd been reading, Your God Is Too Small, *by J.B. Phillips, and as soon as we were off the phone, I ordered a copy. So many of the books in my library were recommended by Dennis that it felt like old times ordering it. I told Dennis about my book, and thanked him for his inspiration and belief in me. Several of the chapters I've written grew out of letters to him.*

The next day, I received an e-mail from Dennis, responding to the chapters that I'd sent to him. He wrote, "I went through them quickly, but they have the Rasmussen flavor—down-to-earth and clear." Reading that, I had to laugh. Dennis had the universe covered, and I was keeping my eyes out down here on Earth.

In the beginning God created the heaven and the earth. And the earth was without form, and void; and darkness was upon the face of the deep. And the Spirit of God moved upon the face of the waters. (Genesis 1:1–2)

And so it began. God is revealed in all that He has created. Being earth-bound, it is hard to comprehend the magnificence of the heavens. We stand here in awe, observing God's handiwork.

It was on a night many years ago when I was out visiting my family in Wisconsin. My parents had gone to bed and I was feeling restless. There not being a whole lot to do in town, I drove out into the country. In the years that had passed since I'd left the Midwest I'd come to appreciate the sky. In New England, our view is often obscured by mountains and forests, and I found that I missed the open vistas of the prairies. As I was driving along, I began to see faint ribbons of colored lights gently flowing across the evening sky. I pulled my car over to the shoulder of the road and stepped out. There was nothing around me but open fields illuminated by the brightest display of the Northern Lights that I'd ever seen. Many years before, I'd sat in the observation dome of an old World War II bomber flying over the Arctic ocean, watching the Northern Lights up close, but nothing compared to that night. As I stood there silently watching the ever-shifting ribbons of color, I felt like I was standing on holy ground. I marveled at the glory of God that was revealed in the prairie sky.

When I drove back to my parent's house, I saw my nephew Mike standing in the street. At the time, he was staying next-door to my parent's house. Even though the tree-lined street partially obscured the view, he was standing there marveling at the sky. He had been driving through the country at the same time I was and like me, he had pulled over to watch the display of light. We stood there together for a few minutes lost in thought before wishing each other a good night and heading inside.

If you're looking for God, you don't have far to go. He reveals himself in everything that we do throughout the most ordinary day. Mountaintop or prairie fields experiences are rare gifts to be savored and remembered. But it is in the valleys of our days where God's presence gives us strength and comfort.

It seems like every time I shop in the store, she's working at the checkout counter. No matter how tired she may be, she always has a smile on her face as she greets the customers approaching her register. The backbone of a store isn't the manager, as some might lead you to believe. It is the person who waits on you. Christ recognized the importance of service, and any job that is done out of a love for the Lord can be a ministry.

"And whosever will be chief among you, let him be your servant: Even as the Son of man came not to be ministered unto, but to minister, and to give his life a ransom for many." (Matthew 20:27–28)

Standing there in line the other day, I watched as a frail, elderly woman slowly placed her few items on the conveyor belt. She appeared to be lost in thought, her mind far away. When the woman at the register saw the woman, she broke into a warm smile and asked her how she was doing. As the woman reached across the counter to take her small packages, they spoke briefly to each other, the checkout clerk expressing her sympathy to the woman at the loss of her husband. It was only a brief moment in time, but I believe it meant a lot to the elderly woman just to know someone cared about her.

When Christ chose his apostles, he didn't select people who were held in the highest esteem. Peter, Andrew, James, and John were simple fishermen. If Jesus came back today and chose apostles, he would look into people's hearts to see the love of his Father dwelling there. He would not be impressed with titles. He might well call a checkout clerk. You know he'd choose some women. He is still calling us to follow him.

If you are looking for God, He's not hard to find. He is in the weed that pushes its way up through a crack in the sidewalk, reminding us of the sanctity of life. He is there in the checkout clerk who stops for a moment to comfort an elderly woman who has just lost her husband. You can see Him in the vastness of the universe He created and hear Him in the silence of a cold mountain lake at sunrise. God is everywhere.

Songs

The Carpenter's Son

Have you heard of a man called Jesus?
The carpenter's son from Galilee
With just one touch, he can heal your body
And he can set your spirit free

CHORUS:
He is my rock, he's my safe harbor
He is my shelter in the storm
When he comes back, I want to go with him
He'll take my hand and lead me home

He will show mercy to the forsaken
He will bring comfort to those who mourn
To the afflicted, he will bring healing
And to the weary, he will bring rest

When the road is dark and dreary
Just when it seems all hope is gone
Call on Jesus, and he will guide you
He'll give you strength to carry on

Brian is twelve years old. He's the son of our neighbors Mike and Nelda. I don't talk with Brian much. Sometimes he will ring our doorbell and politely ask if he and his friends can play basketball in our driveway, using the hoop and backboard we have. He's always

135

very polite and well-mannered, a sweet kid. I imagine that Christ's neighbors thought much the same of him. Jesus didn't ride a skateboard or have a Play Station. His life was much simpler when he was Brian's age. I imagine that his father, Joseph, was already teaching him the craft of working with wood, and whatever toys he had, either he or Joseph most likely made them.

Brian is almost the age that Jesus was when the story of Christ's life is interrupted. The screen goes black when Christ was thirteen, and we don't see him again until he was thirty. In those years, Christ grew to manhood and most likely worked with his father as a carpenter. He had to be a familiar figure in town. People knew him as Jesus, the carpenter's son. But, he wasn't just the carpenter's son. He was God's son. I can't even imagine how difficult it must have been for those who'd watched Jesus growing up to believe that he was the son of God. It would be like Brian telling me when he was thirty that he was the son of God. "What do you mean you're the son of God? You used to shoot baskets in my driveway." That had to be the reaction when word began to spread that Jesus was claiming to be the Messiah.

What a blessing it is for us to know Christ through the scriptures. We know how the story ends. It must have been an enormous test of faith for those who knew Christ as the "kid next door" when he was growing up to accept him as the Messiah. It makes you stop and take a second look at the kid shooting baskets in your driveway.

May I Abide In You

As I lie here on my bed at night
Tossing and turning, Lord, what shall I do?
I pray to Jesus, lead me to the light
May I abide in you

CHORUS:
When I'm weary, Lord give me rest
When I'm lost, show me the way
Cleanse my body and my soul
Grant me another day

I thank you Father for the things you've done
All that I have belongs to you
Thank you for Jesus, your beloved son
May I abide in you

And when my journey here on earth is done
And all of my trials are through
May you praise me for a job well done
May I abide in you

One night, many years ago, I was driving in my car, and started singing one of my favorite songs by The Penguins, best known for their recording of "Earth Angel."

While I stroll through the weary street
Walking and wondering, where can she be?
No, no, no
I know my troubles are not at end[53]

I probably wasn't getting the words quite right, but I've always felt that song from the first time that I heard it. It's definitely a restless heart song. As I often do, I started singing whatever words came into my mind, and the first verse of this song came out. Despite

---

[53] "My Troubles are not at End" by Curtis Williams

137

repeating the line endlessly (an old trick of mine to coax out another verse.) nothing came. It took several more years before the rest of the song came, without warning. I don't even remember how it happened. Maybe I needed to feel the hunger for abiding in Jesus before the Lord gave me the rest of the words.

Songs

Fields of Clover

One thing certain we all know
All things will come to pass
So when the darkness blinds the light
We know it will not last

CHORUS:
For the good old days are still to come
Though the hard times are not over
For we must wear that thorny crown
To walk the fields of clover

Count your blessings while you can
For blessings soon may pass
And though we know not what is to come
Let us toast the half-filled glass

Be your fortune good or bad
There is hope in every day
So for the burdens that we share
Let us lift our voice in praise

I was a child of the Second World War. I was born in 1935 and saw the war through newsreels and the newsreel, *The March of Time*. The music of those war years had a lot to do with how I viewed the war, and one image stood out. Contrasting all the horror of the Holocaust and the returning war veterans who were crippled in mind and spirit were the uplifting, romantic songs of the times. Vera Lynn sang "We'll Meet again," and the Andrew Sisters sang "Don't Sit Under the Apple Tree." The one song that captured all the hope of peace for me was "The White Cliffs of Dover." The imagery in the song fit my vision of heaven far more than the streets of gold and golden slippers in the old gospel songs:

There'll be bluebirds over
The White Cliffs of Dover
Tomorrow
Just you wait and see

There'll be joy and laughter
And peace ever after
Tomorrow
When the world is free[54]

Walking through those fields of clover was as close to heaven on earth as my young mind could imagine.

The other image in this song, "that thorny crown," has equal power. For me, it epitomizes the suffering that Christ endured for us on the cross. When Christ said, "And whosoever doth not bear his cross, and come after me cannot be my disciple" (Luke 14:27), he made it clear that we would have to wear that thorny crown if we wanted to follow him. Both of these images came to mind in writing this song, although it wasn't until much later that I thought at any length about their importance. The song grew out of a general skepticism about focusing too heavily on "the good old days," as if the good times were all over. I find it much better to trust that "the good old days are still to come." That's not to minimize the hard times we will still have to go through. It's an expression of faith that not only will Christ be with us, but that in sharing his thorny crown we will also share his glory in our resurrection.

---

[54] "The White Cliffs of Dover" by Nat Burton and Walter Kent

Songs

Healing Waters

Year after year, he lay by the fountain
Too weak to rise and enter in
When the angel stirred the healing water
He prayed to God, won't you send me a friend

CHORUS:
Lay me down in the healing waters
Cleanse my soul of every sin
Lift me up, that I might walk with thee
Oh Lord, make me whole again

Just when it seemed that all hope was gone
A stranger came to him one day
He said I am the living water
And I will wash all your sins away

And when they asked him who healed his body
Gave him the strength, that he could walk
He did not know the name of Jesus
He only knew he'd been touched by the Lord

This story comes right out of the Bible: "Now there is at Jerusalem by the sheep market a pool, which is called in the Hebrew tongue Bethesda, having five porches. In these lay a great multitude of impotent folk, of blind, halt, withered, waiting for the moving of the water. For an angel went down at a certain season into the pool, and troubled the water; and whosoever then first after the troubling of the water stepped in was made whole of whatsoever disease he had.

"And a certain man was there, which had an infirmity thirty and eight years. When Jesus saw him lie, and knew that he had been now a long time in that case, he saith unto him, 'Wilt thou be made whole?' The impotent man answered him, 'Sir, I have no man, when the water is troubled, to put me into the pool; but while I am coming, another steppeth down before me.'

"Jesus saith unto him 'Rise, take up thy bed and walk.' And

immediately the man was made whole, and took up his bed and walked. And on the same day was the Sabbath. The Jews therefore said unto him that was cured, 'It is the Sabbath day; it is not lawful for thee to carry thy bed.' He answered them, 'He that made me whole, the same said unto me, "Take up thy bed and walk." ' Then asked they him, 'What man is that which said unto thee, "Take up thy bed, and walk?" ' And he that was healed wist not who it was; for Jesus had conveyed himself away, a multitude being in that place" (John 5:2–13).

The man who had waited all those years by the side of the pool was in need of a physical healing. Christ offered much more than that. He is the living water, and he can wash all our sins away.

Earlier in John, Christ makes the distinction between the water that the Samaritan woman came to draw from the well, and the water that he gives: "If thou knewest the gift of God, and who it is that saith to thee, Give me to drink; thou wouldest have asked of him, and he would have given thee living water . . . . Whosoever drinketh of the water that I shall give him shall be in him a well of water springing up into everlasting life" (John 4:10, 14).

We are all in need of healing. Some of us need a physical healing, some a spiritual healing. We carry many old wounds and are burdened down with sins that need to be forgiven so that we can lay them down and walk with Christ in complete freedom. If the man by the pool of Bethesda could wait thirty-eight years for a healing, we can wait on the Lord with complete confidence, knowing that he will lay us down in the healing waters, too.

May My Heart Find Rest in Thee

I take cold comfort in the ways of man
I see no justice in this land
I feel the anger of the un-stayed hand
May my heart find rest in thee

CHORUS:
And in the darkness, give me the eyes of faith
In my sorrow, send down your healing grace
And on my journey, may my path be straight
May my heart find rest in thee

Give me the wisdom that I might understand
Give me the courage, that I might take my stand
And when I'm weary, lend me a helping hand
May my heart find rest in thee

Some spend their lives in a search for power
Ignoring treasures time can't devour
All that I ask in my final hour
May my heart find rest in thee

"These are days of darkness: For behold, the darkness shall cover the earth" (Isaiah 60:2). The evidence of the un-stayed hand is all around us.

You can read it in the papers and the magazines, this world's about to go to hell
Kids are shooting drugs, kids are shooting kids, and things too fierce to tell[55]

---

[55] "Just Because You Like to Do it" by Jerry Rasmussen

In times like these, we turn to the Light of the World, Jesus Christ:

> Then spake Jesus again unto them, saying, I am the light of the world; he that followeth me shall not walk in darkness, but shall have the light of life. (John 8:12)

This song is a prayer. It has lifted me in times of darkness, though not a note was sung. Our only way to see in the darkness is through the eyes of faith, leaning on Jesus. Only he can give our hearts rest.

Just Because You Like To Do It, That Don't Make It Right

God come to Noah, late one day, said, Son, I got a job for you
I'm getting mighty tired of these people 'round here doin' what
  they want to do
I've told them once, I've told them twice
They never want to listen to my advice
So build yourself a boat, and get on out of here before it rains

CHORUS:
Now, I ain't been to heaven, but I've been told
The streets up there, are lined with gold
I ain't been to hell, but from what I hear
It can get mighty hot down there

So you better mind your manners, watch your P's and Q's
'Cause you don't know when God's watching you
And just because you like to do it, that don't make it right

God sent Jonah across the sea in the belly of a whale
He sent him on down to Nineveh, and he lived to tell the tale
He told them people, better mind your ways
You better get ready for the judgment day
And just because you like to do it, that don't make it right

Now you can read it in the papers and the magazines, this
  world's about to go to hell
Kids are shooting drugs, kids are shooting kids, and things too
  fierce to tell
You can do what you do, you can say what you say
But you better get ready for the judgment day
And just because you like to do it, that don't make it right

The "Father" of gospel music, Thomas A Dorsey, didn't start out singing for the Lord. He recorded country blues under the name of Georgia Tom. Some of the songs he sang were on the risqué side. After he accepted Jesus Christ as his Savior, some of that old blues got mixed in with the gospel songs he was writing. Over the years, many other blues singers have also sang gospel. It depended on where they were at the time. Little Richard had a round-trip ticket from rhythm and blues to gospel, and then back to rhythm and blues.

This song, in structure and chord progression, is very much a country blues song, with a touch of ragtime thrown in. But the lyrics are gospel in topic, with a wry look at our fallacies, when we claim to be serving the Lord, when we're just pleasing ourselves. Not everything that we enjoy doing (including things that we say we are doing for the Lord) are right. We just enjoy doing them.

Jerusalem Slim

You could find him by the campfires late at night
Or wading in the water in the morning light
He always took the time to lend a hand
He was kind of slow moving for a traveling man

CHORUS:
No sooner did he come than he'd be gone
And he never had a home to call his own
So when you get in trouble you can call on him
'Cause you never had a friend like Jerusalem Slim

Jerusalem Slim, he was long and tall
And every down-and-outer, well, he knew them all
And even though he never had a dime to lend
He never met a man he didn't call a friend

Now living on the road it ain't nothing new
So when you need a hand, just to get you through
When you're feeling down and you're all alone
He knows all about it, 'cause he's walked that road

A woman I worked with brought me an article that she'd clipped out of the newspaper. She thought that there might be material for a song in it. The article was about the difference between hobos, tramps, and bums.

Hobos spend much of their lives on the road. They live from day to day, picking up work wherever they can find it. Even though they are usually penniless, they take pride in working for their food. During the depression, hobos traveled the country by hitching a ride on a passing freight train. Tramps are equally penniless and are as homeless as hobos. Unlike hobos, they avoid work like the plague and are more likely to travel on foot. Bums are the next step down in the hierarchy of the penniless. They don't travel or work. They pretty much stay in one place, and live by panhandling on the streets.

At one point in their lives, some well-known people lived as hobos, among them: Woody Guthrie, Jack Dempsey, Jack Kerouac,

Jack London, Robert Mitchum, Eugene O'Neil, and John Steinbeck. But the most famous of all hobos was Jesus Christ. He fit the description perfectly. In the years of his ministry, he was constantly traveling (although not by catching a freight train). The only home he knew was the road:

> And Jesus saith unto them, The foxes have holes, and the birds of the air have nests; but the Son of man hath no where to lay his head. (Matthew 8:20)

Like any good hobo, Christ was willing to work for food. He didn't chop wood or clean out the barn. His work was salvation. The hobos understood this, and because they figured that he never knew where his next meal was coming from, he was probably slim: Jerusalem Slim.

When I Get To Glory

It's a long and a lonesome journey
On a rough and a rocky road
It's not made for the weak or the faint of heart
You have to carry such a heavy load

CHORUS:
He's going to meet me
*   Jesus' going to meet me there*
I'm going to sit down
*   Sit down in the welcome chair*
He's going to greet me
* Jesus' going to shake my hand*
He's going to tell me
*   Tell me so I'll understand*
I'm going to lay down
*   Lay my heavy burden down*
I'll hear the angels
*   Singing with the sweetest sound*
When I get to glory, glory be
What a great day that will be

I'm going to see my Mother
You know she died so long ago
What a blessed, sweet reunion
When I meet her on that shore

I don't know about those streets of gold up there
I don't know about those starry crowns
I don't need no golden slippers, Lord
I just want to walk around

I'm living on the promise of my Savior
Jesus Christ my Lord
The train to Glory will be leaving soon
You know it's time to get on board

In black Baptist churches, funerals are often uplifting. While there is grieving at the loss of a loved one, there's also rejoicing. Upbeat, energetic songs are a reflection of the joy that the deceased is experiencing, having gone home. When the musician Eric Clapton lost his young son in a tragic accident, he dealt with the pain by writing a beautiful song, "Tears in Heaven."

In the Book of Revelation, John describes a new Jerusalem, where God will wipe away our every tear.

> And I saw a new heaven and a new earth; for the first heaven and the first earth were passed away; and there was no more sea. And I John saw the holy city, new Jerusalem, coming down from God out of heaven, prepared as a bride adorned for her husband . . . . And God shall wipe away all tears from their eyes; and there shall be no more death, neither sorrow nor crying, neither shall there be any more pain; for the former things are passed away. (Revelation 21:1–2, 4)

When we get to glory, it will indeed be a great day!

I'll Be Home

When I come to the place where my Master awaits
Then I know I'll be home
When I meet him there, my joy he will share
And I'll never be alone

There's a dark road ahead that I wearily tread
And the night is cold
But his face I can see, and it beckons to me
And I believe all I've been told

Though temptation is great, I will not turn away
I must journey on
For the end is near, and death holds no fear
For I know what lies beyond

All my sorrow and pain will not be in vain
When I reach my goal
When he takes my hand, then I'll understand
And his love will cleanse my soul

I wrote this song under the influence—the influence of *Lord of the Rings* by J.R.R. Tolkien and an old hymn, "My Long Journey Home," from a recording by Doc Watson. They both conjured up images of a long journey through darkness, even though the goals were very different. The face that Frodo Baggins saw was not the comforting image of Jesus Christ.

Having seen the beauty of my mother's long journey home, I know now that Christ's face makes all the difference in the world. Death may be a long journey, but it is not taken alone.

Jesus, Move on the Water

I woke up Monday morning,
My heart was filled with pain
Another long-time friend was gone
And he never once blessed your name

CHORUS:
Jesus, move on the water
Reach out your loving hand
Another poor soul is sinking down
Won't you help him to take his stand

Some are lost in their evil ways
Some are drowned in sin
Some just need a helping hand
Oh Lord, won't you take them in

Jesus walked on the water
Moses parted the sea
You can walk on the water, too
If only you believe

Some songs are prayers. This one came in a rush. While it was very much of the moment, the prayer is one that remains on my lips. It is lifted up for all those who are suffering through a dark time in their lives, who do not know Jesus, or God. It is a cry to Jesus to reach out his loving hand. It is a prayer for all of us.

Last Chance for Salvation

There's a sign in the courtyard in front of the church
Last Chance for Salvation, Service Today
There's a sign in the bar says "Cold Miller on Tap"
Where the dreams of a lifetime go drifting away

CHORUS:
Some turn to Jesus, some turn to the bottle
Some find redemption, some find nothing at all
Some wait a lifetime for a prayer to be answered
Some climb marble stairways, some sleep in the hall

The angels in hymns all wear beautiful robes
With voices as sweet as an innocent child
The Honky-tonk angels, their voices are rough
But they offer their comforts, if just for awhile

If Jesus should come back, just for a day
To preach on that corner to all who pass by
Who'd stop and listen, and who'd walk away?
And turn from salvation and never know why

This song grew out of my remembrances of my growing-up days in southern Wisconsin. Zoning laws being what they are these days, I don't know if they'd allow a bar to be built directly across the street from a church. Both the bar and the church are long since gone. But the memories remain.

The battle between good and not so good raged nightly on the streets of Janesville. In no place was that more obvious than on the corner of Main and Wall Street. On one side of the street in a large, modern, salmon-colored building, an army of Christian Soldiers gathered at the Salvation Army, poised and ready to march off to war. Directly across the street in an old, rundown building was Planter's Hotel. On street level in Planter's Bar, Pabst Blue Ribbon ruled the kingdom and Hank Williams was the high priest.

Friday afternoon, with paychecks tucked in the shirt pockets of their bib overalls, a legion of men descended on Planter's Bar for a liquid dinner and a few games of Euchre. One drink led to another, and by the time the bar closed at one in the morning, most of the men couldn't walk a crooked line, let alone a straight one. My father worshipped regularly at Planter's Bar and sometimes wouldn't make it home until Monday afternoon when he came home from work, spending the weekend hunting or fishing. And making Mister Pabst a wealthy man.

Growing up, I never understood the lure of the bars in town. All that I knew was that they kept my father away from home most weekends, and I felt cheated. A family in our neighborhood was very involved with the Salvation Army, and I went with them many times to see old movies they'd show at night, or to social gatherings. The contrast between the freshly scrubbed faces and enthusiasm of the people at the Salvation Army and the worn-out, tired-looking, end-of-week, thank-God-it's-over crowd hunched over at the bar at Planter's was striking. It took growing up and making peace with Mr. Pabst and my father for me to see that both places of worship had their goodness and pleasure, along with their failings. And later in life, my father found greater nourishment in a pew than sitting at a bar. It took writing a few songs for me to find that peace. This was one of them.

A Sweet, Quiet Peace

Storms may rage, and dark clouds gather
Sometimes my way is hard to see
But in my heart, there's a calm assurance
Because I know that he walks with me

CHORUS:
One thing I know, and this for certain
All will be well no matter what the future holds
He will be there to share my every burden
And there's a sweet, quiet peace in my soul

Peter walked upon the water
When he heard our Savior call
Just keep your eye on Christ our Savior
He will never let you fall

When your heart is heavy laden
And your strength is almost gone
Give your heart to Christ our Savior
He'll give you strength to carry on

Peace comes quietly. It gives us a calm assurance in our hearts. After all the shouting, testifying, and full-throttle music dies down, peace gets you over in the corner. Peace is not dramatic. It doesn't have a whole lot to say, and like God, it speaks in a "still, small voice." You can't track it down or corner it. You have to wait patiently and let it come to you. I leave you with this promise from Christ:

Peace I leave with you, my peace I give unto you; not as the world giveth, give I unto you. (John 14:27)

About the Author

For the last forty five years, Jerry Rasmussen has been writing folk and gospel songs, and performing on his own and with his gospel quartet, The Gospel Messengers. He has sung from Thespian Hall in Boonville, Missouri, to Town Hall in New York City. Jerry's songs have appeared in print in *Sing Out!* magazine and in *New Folk Favorites: 45 of the best songs of today's singer/ songwriters* published by Hal Leonard Publishing Company. He was featured in a half-hour concert for New York State public television as part of their *In the Tradition* series and has performed on many other television programs. He has five CDs to his credit, including one with the Gospel Messengers, and his songs have been recorded by more than a dozen other musicians and groups.

Jerry earned a B.S. and M.S. degree in Geology at the University of Wisconsin and worked for two years toward a Doctorate at Columbia University. He served on the faculty of Hunter College in New York City for two years. For thirty years he was Executive Director of the Stamford Museum and Nature Center in Stamford, Connecticut.

Mr. Rasmussen performs regularly in churches, concerts, folk festivals, nursing homes, and health care centers. He has always written, and has had articles published in various folk newsletters and publications. His writings on faith go back as far as his song-writing.

DISCOGRAPHY

Get Down Home – Folk Legacy Records CD77
The Secret Life of Jerry Rasmussen – Folk Legacy Records CD101
Handful of Songs – Jack Rabbit 1
Without That Night – The Gospel Messengers – Jackrabbit 2
Back When I Was Young – Jackrabbit 3

CONTACT:
Jerry Rasmussen
95 Hillcrest Ave.
Derby, CT 06418
203-736-0296
www.jrasmussen.net

Printed in the United States
146976LV00001B/5/P

9 781432 736767